Leabharlann Chontae Luimn

Irish Oyster Cuisine

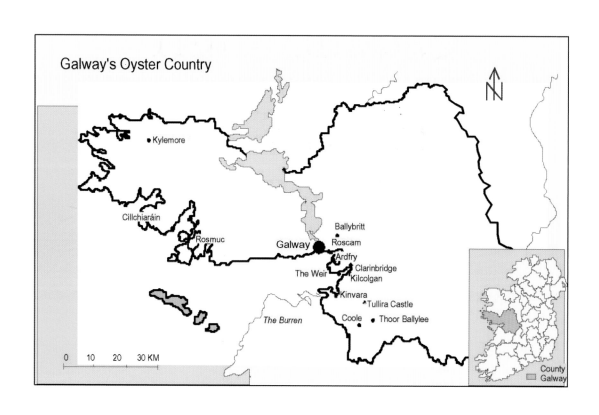

Galway's Oyster Country

Kylemore

Cillchiaráin

Rosmuc

Galway

Ballybritt

Roscam

Ardfry

Clarinbridge

The Weir

Kilcolgan

Kinvara

Tullira Castle

The Burren

Coole

Thoor Ballylee

0   10   20   30 KM

County
Galway

Irish Oyster Cuisine
Cuisine Oisrí

Máirín Uí Chomáin

A. & A. Farmar

British Library cataloguing in Publication Data
A CIP catalogue record for this book is available from the
British Library.

The publishers would like to thank the sponsors
Bord Iascaigh Mhara and Foras na Gaeilge, neither of whom however is responsible
in any way for the contents of this book.

This project has been part-funded by Galway Rural Development Company Ltd.
under the NRDP. GRD cannot accept responsibility for omissions or inaccuracies
contained therein.

Picture credits: BIM 19, 112; Walter Pfeiffer 1, 3, 31, 36, 44, 52, 60, 68, 84, 88, 93, 100, 105, 108; Galway International Oyster Festival 71, 98; Galway Public Library 38, 42, 74, 77

Cover design by Cobalt
Text edited, designed and set by A. & A. Farmar
Printed and bound in Spain by GraphyCems

ISBN 1-899047-85-9

First published in 2004
by
A. & A. Farmar
Beech House, 78 Ranelagh Village
Dublin 6, Ireland
Tel: 353 1 496 3625 Fax: 353 1 497 0107
Email: afarmar@iol.ie Web: farmarbooks.com

To Patrick and the four pearls in my
life—Fiona, Ríona, Cormac and Treasa

Do Phádraig agus mo pheárlaí féin—
Fiona, Ríona, Cormac agus Treasa

Contents

Acknowledgements

I owe enormous debts of gratitude to many people for their help and encouragement over the past few years.

The publishers, Tony and Anna Farmar, always remained enthusiastic and supportive. They were ably assisted by Myra Dowling and by the editing skills of Pat Carroll. A special word of thanks is due to my financial sponsors: Bord Iascaigh Mhara and its staff, especially Orlaith O Callaghan and Chief Executive Pat Keogh; Galway Rural Development Company Ltd, particularly Elaine Quinn; and Foras na Gaeilge, where Deirdre Davitt was most helpful.

Colleagues in the Irish Food Writers Guild were always ready to offer professional advice. Honor Moore provided great inspiration; Nuala Cullen took much time to help with the testing of recipes, as did Phena O'Boyle.

Useful information on oyster production came from an t-Ollamh Pádraic Ó Céidigh and Professor Noël Wilkins at NUI Galway. An t-Ollamh Micheál Ó Cinnéide and Dr Siubhán Comer at the University's Department of Geography supplied the map of Galway's oyster country.

Several people contributed to the book's photography. To Walter Pfeiffer goes the credit for the excellent pictures of oystering and oyster dishes, and to his food stylist, Erica Jane Ryan, for setting out the dishes with elegance. Maureen Moran sourced photographs from Galway County Library; Pádraic Ó hAoláin at Údarás na Gaeltachta also provided photographs. John Rabbitt of the Galway Oyster Festival Committee granted permission to use some shots from earlier festivals. Marie Mannion at the Galway Heritage Centre was a mine of information on local history in the county. Joe Steve Ó Neachtain celebrated the oyster with his inimitable poetic imagination.

My good friend Máire Ní Thuathail spent long hours with me in the kitchen, sampling my creations. I was fortunate to get Martin Moran MW to contribute informative notes on serving wine with oysters. Karen Hughes provided much valued secretarial support.

My thanks to producers and suppliers of shellfish: Brian Martyn, Michael Irwin, James and Diarmuid Keane, Michael Kelly and Willie Moran. Samples of seaweed and information on sea vegetables came from Máirtín Walsh, Manus McGonigle, Tom Sally Ó Flatharta and Páraic Mac Donncha. James Harrington introduced Walter Pfeiffer to the underwater life of Kilkieran Bay.

A final word of thanks goes to my own family, immediate and extended, who must have often wondered where and when it would all end. My husband, Patrick, remained patient and most helpful even in the midst of unavoidable domestic chaos that went with recipe testing, cooking and writing. Again, my sincere gratitude to all and to many other friends for their kindness.

Buíochas

Mar a fhásann an t–oisre mór ón sceathrach beag bídeach ar ghrinneall na farraige, d'fhás an leabhar seo as smaoineamh beag bídeach i m'intinn, agus le mórchuid cabhrach.

Tá mé thar a bheith buíoch de na foilsitheoirí, Tony agus Anna Farmar, faoina gcúnamh agus a ndíograis agus de Myra Dowling, agus de Pat Carroll faoina gcuid scileanna eagarthóireachta.

Tá buíochas ar leith dlite dóibh sin a rinne urraíocht airgeadais ar an saothar: Bord Iascaigh Mhara, go háirithe Órlaith O'Callaghan, agus an Príomhfheidhmeanach Pat Keogh; Galway Rural Develepment Company Ltd, go háirithe Elaine Quinn; Foras na Gaeilge, áit ar chabhraigh Deirdre Davitt go mór liom a chinntiú go mbeadh leathshliogán, ar a laghad, den oisre dúchais le fáil sa teanga dhúchais.

Bhí mo chairde san Irish Foodwriters Guild fial flaithiúil liom; chaith Nuala Cullen go leor ama ag cabhrú liom ag tástáil na n–oideas, rud a rinne Phena O'Boyle freisin.

Roinn an tOllamh Pádraig Ó Céidigh agus an tOllamh Noël Wilkins ó Ollscoil Náisiúnta na hÉireann Gaillimh a gcuid eolais faoi shíolrú agus táirgiú oisrí go fial liom. Chuir an tOllamh Mícheál Ó Cinnéide agus Dr Siubhán Comer ó Roinn na Tíreolaíochta san ollscoil chéanna, mapa ar fáil dom de cheantar oisrí na Gaillimhe.

Chabhraigh daoine éagsúla liom leis na grianghraif. Is é Walter Pfeiffer a thóg na pictiúir bhreátha de na hoisrí ina ndreacha éagsúla, agus is í Erica Jane Ryan a chóirígh go snasta na miasa. Chuir Maureen Moran ó Leabharlann an Chontae, Gaillimh, agus Pádraic Ó hAoláin ó Údaras na Gaeltachta pictiúir eile chugam. Thug John Rabbitt ó Choiste Fhéile na nOisrí cead dom pictiúir ó na féilte atá caite a úsáid. Fuair mé réimsí eolais faoi stair áitiúil ar fud an chontae ó Marie Mannion ó Lárionad Oidhreachta na Gaillimhe. Mhol Joe Steve Ó Neachtain an t-oisre le na dhán úrnua.

Tá mé go mór faoi chomaoin ag mo chara, Máire Ní Thuathail, a chaith go leor ama sa chistin liom ag blaiseadh na n-oideas. Bhí an t-ádh orm gur roinn Martin Moran, Máistir Fíona, a chuid eolais go flaithiúil liom. Chabhraigh Karen Hughes go héifeachtach ó thaobh rúnaíochta de.

Ní fhéadfainn dóthain buíochais a ghlacadh leis na soláthróirí iasc sliogánach: Brian Martyn, Michael Irwin, James agus Diarmuid Keane, Michael Kelly agus Willie Moran.

Fuair mé fios feamaine agus glasraí mara ó Mhártín Walsh, Manus McGonigle, Tom Sally Ó Flatharta agus Páraic Mac Donncha. Thug James Harrington go grineal farraige Walter Pfeiffer chun scoth na bpictiúirí do oisrí Chill Chiaráin a thógáil.

Agus, ar deireadh, ba mhaith liom buíochas a ghabháil le mo chlann, a mbeidh áthas orthu go bhfuil an obair seo tugtha chun críche. Thug m'fhear, Pádraig, cúnamh go fial agus go foighneach dom, tríd an gcíréb go léir a bhain leis na hoidis a thástáil agus a chur ar phár. Buíochas ar leith le duine ar bith a chabhraigh liom agus nach bhfuil luaite.

Máirín Uí Chomáin

Oisre

Tíolacthaí na farraige
a shíolraigh
i mbroinn na sliogán.
Gan cócaireacht
ag teastáil uaidh,
ach é a oscailt
is a shlogadh.
Blas a' tsáile
de bheadaíocht air,
ag tabhairt spreacadh duit
is anáil.
Tá péarla
ó ghrinneall farraige
blasta fuar is folláin.

Joe Steve Ó Neachtain
Bealtaine 2004

Seo dán omóis don oisre ó pheann cruthaitheach Joe Steve Ó Neachtain as an Spidéal. Tá an iomad gradaim bronnta ar Joe dhá chuid drámaí in a measc: gradam Jacob's, gradam Litríochta Chló Iar-Chonnachta faoí dhó, freisin duais Oireachtais agus duais Stuart Parker/ BBC Radio Uladh.

Introduction

Since my earliest days the sea has coaxed me. From the back steps of my childhood home in Connemara, I could literally dip my toes in the waters of Galway Bay. Exploring the seashore and its many forms of life through daily and seasonal change became a source of pleasure and constant wonder. One of our clan, Seamus Mac An Iomaire, had published *Cladaigh Chonamara*, an excellent guide. It was also a revelation to me that features of our humble surroundings could be the basis for a book. Although I did not realise it then, this was an early inspiration to myself to discover more about our maritime heritage and even write about the shellfish and carrageen which were part of the family diet.

Later, as a young home economist I had, as one of my first assignments, the task of training young Aran fishermen to cook well for themselves during their long stays at sea. With marriage came a move to Dublin and, for a while, to the US. In the US I saw how well various ethnic groups treasured their own native dishes, a clear hint that the island of Ireland could be more imaginative in using its seafood resources.

Passing years, more changes of location and family commitments made for a jagged career path, but provided for many fulfilling experiences in teaching, commercial food advisory services, catering and the media. Gradually, but irresistibly, those early and vague thoughts of writing 'something about sea foods' firmed up into an exciting project on oyster cuisine. Then, more recently, fortune favoured me once more when I was able to return again and set up home within an oar's length of the Galway shoreline—the ideal setting to complete the circle and bring a journey of a long process of thought to finality. There you have much of the context and stimulus for the content and format of this cookbook.

Irish oysters are found in some great oyster beds around our coasts and all are worthy of celebration. Granting that, I felt it was essential to link my ideas on oyster cuisine to the part of the coast which I know best—that from Cleggan down to Kinvara. Apart from the obvious practicalities, I have another reason for this. In these days of global food chains and of placeless products, it seems important to be able to link foods to their places of origin. And these places are not mere locations on a map; they each have their own characteristics, their different associations with the past, and their own local personalities. So, most of the recipes here are named after places or people in Galway's oyster country, with vignettes on the selections I have made. In that spirit and to emphasise the Irishness of our oysters, I have presented these descriptions in Irish also. Irish is, of course, the everyday language in some of Galway's oyster producing areas, and my own first language.

Enjoying oysters

Now about the book's cuisine. Again, to give a little more context, there is precious little written about oyster cooking in Ireland. This is a pity and indeed strange when we realise that oysters were enjoyed by ancient Greeks, Roman Emperors and the Chinese of old. Among Irish people, they were a common food for centuries until supplies were diminished through over-fishing and coastal developments.

Happily, we now produce thousands of tonnes annually, mainly for the French market. Why not enjoy them to a greater extent ourselves? Oysters are rich in iodine, phosphorus and zinc, all of which add nutritional value to a diet. Any dining establishment presenting this delicacy must surely take pride in other aspects of its menu.

We commonly think of consuming oysters by eating them raw in their half shells, washing them down with a few draughts of a good Irish beverage. In this way, they are indeed a treat. But can I entice you to be a little more venturesome? Oysters are very versatile in their culinary uses and can be enjoyed in a variety of settings—at breakfast, lunch, brunch, supper and as finger food at any time of the day. Here, I show quite a number of possibilities for cooking and presenting oysters. The recipes are not difficult. I suggest you start with the soups—they are intended to get you hooked with their strong briny flavour.

The natural complements

To complement the oyster, I introduce some breads in which seaweeds are used as an ingredient. Seaweed is an abundant natural resource which continually regenerates itself; it is one of the earliest forms of plant life on the planet and is a basis for a wide range of useful products. Ireland is fortunate in having an extensive coastline of over 3,000 kilometres, much of it on the Atlantic seaboard. A mix of exposed open coast, rocky bays and smaller inlets offers ideal conditions for seaweed growth. The west coast waters are among the cleanest in the world and are a source of seaweed of the highest quality. Marine scientists will tell us that over 500 different species of Irish coast seaweed have been identified. For centuries Irish seaweed has been used as a fertiliser, and indeed marine plants have also been harvested for food and cosmetic purposes.

Carrageen is the most important of all our seaweeds as a remedy for colds and flu, as a pick me up drink on cold winter days when cooked in milk (or water) strained, sweetened and sometimes flavoured with lemon, honey, cinnamon or nutmeg. Adults, of course, flavour it with some good Irish whiskey.

When growing up in Connemara we picked carrageen at low tide, then spread it on land and turned it a few times until its dark colour was bleached white by sun, rain showers and wind. My mother Kate, God rest her now, was very imaginative in using the dried carrageen in desserts and milk drinks. The name is Irish and it means 'little rock' or *'carraigín'*.

Carrageen is used a lot in the health and beauty industry now as a source of carrageenan, a substance which has gelling properties similar to agar-agar, as a natural stabiliser. I would rate carrageen as one of our very own Irish desserts and cold remedies. It can be enjoyed by young and old, and it is also a fantastic thickening agent for soups and stews. It should be on many more Irish menus. I use it dampened and as a bed to sit my raw native oysters on and then recycle and cook it after! I find it a conversation piece and many overseas visitors have never seen or heard of it.

From the seashore we also gathered dulse, which we called *creathnach* in Irish. When dried, dulse had a sweet taste and we simply chewed it like today's chewing gum, or cooked it in milk as a kind of stew. I use it chopped raw into salads, snipped and added to mashed potatoes, scrambled eggs, stews and sauces, blanched and chopped in savoury breads, sometimes deep fried as a garnish or again as a bed for oysters as it has wonderful colours of purple and deep crimson.

Carrageen and dulse are very nutritious. The older people recognised this and considered these seaweeds essential in fighting winter colds and curing many ailments. No wonder they were in keen demand in the old country markets. I am happy to say that carrageen and dulse can still be purchased in health food stores.

It is a pleasure for me to see the folk foods of old finding a rightful place in modern cooking and dining. My hope is that this cookbook will strengthen the links between these two worlds.

Réamhrá

Tá mé faoi dhraíocht ag an bhfarraige ó bhí mé an-óg. Thagadh an lán mara ag lapadaíl go leac an dorais againn i gConamara nuair a bhí mé i mo chailín beag, agus b'aoibhinn liom a bheith ag siúl le cladach agus ag tabhairt faoi deara an chaoi a n-athraíodh an fharraige a dreach ó lá go lá agus ó shéasúr go séasúr. Nuair a léigh mé an leabhar álainn sin Cladaí Chonamara a scríobh Séamus Mac Con Iomaire, (fear de mo shloinne féin, dála an scéil) mhéadaigh ar an draíocht. B'fhéidir gurb é sin a chéad spreag mé, i ngan fhios dom féin, le staidéar níos grinne a dhéanamh ar an iasc sliogánach agus ar an gcarraigín a d'itheadh muid go minic sa mbaile.

Nuair a cháiligh mé i mo mhúinteoir eacnamaíocht bhaile, fuair mé mo chéad phost i gCill Rónáin, áit a raibh mé ag traenáil iascairí óga Árann le béilí blasta a réiteach dóibh féin ar bord loinge ar bharr toinne. Nuair a phós mé níos deireanaí, d'aistrigh mé go Baile Átha Cliath agus ina dhiaidh sin go Stáit Aontaithe Mheiriceá ar feadh seal blianta, áit a bhfaca mé an meas a bhí ag grúpaí eitneacha ar bhia agus ar chócaireacht a dtíre dúchais féin. Rith sé liom go bhféadfadh muintir na hÉireann i bhfad níos mó úsáide a bhaint as ár mbia mara, agus níos mó samhlaíochta a úsáid á chócaráil.

Le himeacht na mblianta, de réir mar fuair mé taithí múinteoireachta agus comhairleoireachta bia, ar fud na tíre agus sna meáin chumarsáide, d'fhás an smaoineamh i mo cheann go scríobhfainn rud éigin faoi bhia mara. De réir a chéile shocraigh mé díriú go hiomlán ar chócaireacht oisrí. Ansin, le gairid, bhí sé d'ádh orm go bhfuair mé an deis cur fúm go buan ar chósta thiar na tíre arís, áit a bhfuil mé anois ag breathnú amach ar Chuan na Gaillimhe. Bhí a fhios agam ansin go raibh an t-am tagtha le tabhairt faoin togra i ndáiríre.

Is mar sin, a bheag nó a mhór, a tháinig an leabhar cócaireachta seo ar an saol. Tá an t-oisre Éireannach le fáil ar bheirtreacha cáiliúla timpeall an chósta, ach shocraigh mise díriú ar an gcuid sin de chósta na Gaillimhe a bhfuil aithne mhaith agam féin air, ón gCloigeann thiar go Cinn Mhara thoir. Ach tá fáth eile leis seo. Tá na hollchomhlachtaí domhanda bia chomh cumhachtach sin sa lá atá inniu ann go bhfuil tábhacht níos mó ná riamh anois, dar liom, le fios a bheith ag duine cár fhás an bia atá ar a phláta. Agus tá níos mó ná an suíomh ar an mapa i gceist, mar tá a stair agus a seanchas agus a bpearsantacht féin ag na beirtreacha éagsúla agus ag na bailte lena dtaobh. Sin é an fáth go bhfuil formhór na n-oideas sa leabhar seo ainmnithe i ndiaidh áiteacha áirithe nó tiomnaithe agam do dhaoine áirithe i gceantar oisrí na Gaillimhe. Tá roinnt mhaith den cheantar céanna sin suite i nGaeltacht Chonamara, áit a bhfuil an Ghaeilge, mo theanga dhúchais féin, á labhairt leis na cianta.

Bhí tóir ar na hoisrí riamh anall ag na Sínigh, ag na Gréagaigh agus ag Impirí na Róimhe, agus gnáthbhia a bhí iontu in Éirinn i gcaitheamh na gcéadta bliain, nó gur éiríodar gann de bharr ró-iascach agus forbairt cois cósta. Is mór an t-ionadh, mar sin, a laghad atá scríofa faoi chócaireacht oisrí in Éirinn. Táirgíonn muid na mílte tonna oisrí sa tír seo faoi láthair, ach is ar mhargadh na Fraince is mó a díoltar iad. Ba cheart do mhuintir na hÉireann féin níos mó oisrí a ithe, mar tá íodáin, sinc agus fosfar go fairsing iontu, rud a fhágann cothú maith iontu mar bhia. Bialann ar bith a chuireann oisrí ar a mbiachlár, bíonn bród acu de ghnáth as an gcuid eile dá mbiachlár freisin.

Is iondúil go smaoinítear ar oisrí agus iad á n-ithe amh as a leathshliogáin, agus deoch mhaith Éireannach á caitheamh siar in éineacht leo. Is deas an bealach é, ach ní hé an t-aon bhealach é le sásamh a bhaint as oisrí. Níl aon deire leis an oiread bealaí chun oisrí a ithe, ó thus na maidne le bricfeasta go deire oíche mar shuipéar, nó am ar bith mar bhia méire. Tá roinnt bealaí difriúla sa leabhar seo le hoisrí a chócaráil, agus níl na hoidis deacair le réiteach. Molaim, mar sin féin, go dtosófá leis an anraith, mar go meallfaidh blas goirt na farraige thú le tabhairt faoi na hoidis eile.

Tá aráin ar leith molta agam chun dul leis na hoisrí, aráin ina gcuirtear cineálacha éagsúla feamainne. Nuair a bhí mé ag fás suas i gConamara, bhain muid agus thriomaigh muid carraigín. Bhí mo mháthair, Kate, go ndéana Dia trócaire uirthi, an-mhaith á bhruith ar bhainne agus ag déanamh milseog as. Bhain muid creathnach nó duileasc sa gcladach freisin agus thriomaigh muid í; bhruith muid ar bhainne í, nó chogain muid í mar dhéanfá le guma coganta. Tá cothú maith i gcarraigín agus i gcreathnach, rud a thuig an mhuintir a tháinig romhainn, mar gur thógadar iad mar leigheas ar shlaghdán agus ar ghalair éagsúla. Bhíodh éileamh mór orthu sna seanmhargaí tuaithe, agus ní haon ionadh go bhfuil fáil orthu i gcónaí sna siopaí sláinte.

Is deas an rud a fheiceáil go bhfuil áit fós ag bia na seanmhuintire i gcócaireacht agus i mbialanna na linne seo. Tá súil agam go neartóidh an leabhar seo an ceangal idir an saol atá imithe agus an saol atá anois ann.

Notes on oysters

Cultivation and types

Oysters have been in the seas for millions of years. Normally static creatures, they live in colonies where the base is firm enough to support their weight, and where water temperatures and planktonic food resources are suitable. The traditional methods of harvesting are hand-picking in shallow water, or dredging by dragging a metal frame behind a boat. On modern shellfish farms where oysters are grown in bags attached to trestles, harvesting work is less laborious.

Two types of oysters are now cultivated in Ireland. The native European or flat oyster (*Ostrea edulis*) is seasonal. It spawns during the summer months and hence is available only when there is an 'R' in the month. To provide for all year round cultivation, and supplement the native production, the Pacific or cupped rock oyster (*Crassostrea gigas*) was introduced in the 1970s. Irish water temperatures are too cool for gigas to spawn here, but young oysters are provided in hatcheries and we therefore have the luxury of the cupped or gigas oyster throughout the whole year.

The native variety normally takes up to five years to grow and mature to harvestable size, while the Pacific type reaches this stage in 18–28 months.

The latter are grown on structures placed at low tide mark and at a density far higher than the native oyster.

Oysters, like cows and sheep, are vegetarians which turn plant food into flesh. But the plants the oysters consume are so small that they must be filtered from the water by means of delicate net membranes called gills. Since the microscopic plants of the sea cost nothing and the oyster can convert them into oyster meat with great efficiency, the oyster is considered a good 'animal' to grow on a sea farm.

Oysters are one of our best health foods, being low in calories and highly nutritious. They are high in calcium and in vitamins A and D. As a good source of selenium and zinc, they have the reputation for enhancing fertility. They also help to produce serotonin, a chemical that helps to regulate sleep and appetite, and to fight infection. Such a nutrient-rich food offers a better basis for health than relying on supplements.

Buying and storing oysters

Despite their robust appearance, oysters are perishable creatures. As live molluscs they must be protected against damage and contamination, and must not be exposed to extreme temperatures. When buying, ensure that they are tightly closed, or that they close quickly when lightly tapped. They are sensitive to being dropped onto hard surfaces or other such impact damage. Shells should not be damaged or broken; this adversely affects the quality.

Store oysters with the flat shell uppermost to retain the juices. They should be closely packed and kept at a low temperature in a cool place, preferably in the dark and in a moist container or covered with a damp cloth. The bottom of the fridge is ideal for storage. Properly stored, oysters will keep for up to a week in winter and up to four days in summer.

Did you know?

Oysters produce pearls. They have an inner layer of shell made of a lustrous substance called nacre.

How to open an oyster

If a bit of foreign matter gets into the shell, such as a grain of sand, the oyster will coat it gradually with layers of nacre or mother of pearl, isolating it from the fleshy part. As the oyster matures, this is formed into a pearl. But do not raise your hopes. Relatively few oysters will happen to have pearls; even fewer will produce gems.

Oysters change sex quite frequently, the native showing more agility than the Pacific in this regard. This confusing characteristic moved Galwayman Henry Comerford to compose the following at a Galway Oyster Festival:

The amorous oyster

Bisexual the oyster is,
and cannot tell its her from his,
And goes a-courting every day,
With him or her or even they;
But your oyster squeals when firmly bit,
'Please! I'm not him or her: I'm it.'

Using an oyster knife (or stubby bladed knife) insert the point at the hinge of the oyster and slip the knife slightly down and across, close to the top of the shell (this cuts the muscle from the shell). Slide the knife under the body of the oyster and cut the muscle attaching it to the deep bottom shell. The oyster can then be easily removed for eating or cooking.

Nótaí faoi oisrí

Saothrú an dá chineál

Tá oisrí ag fás sna farraigí leis na milliún bliain, agus is gnách leo fanacht san áit chéanna i gcaitheamh a saoil. Maireann siad i gcomhluadair mhóra ar ghrinneall réidh atá sách crua lena meáchan a iompar, agus in uiscí ina bhfuil dóthain teochta agus dóthain planctóin. Pioctar le láimh iad in uiscí tanaí, nó is féidir iad a dhreideáil as bád le fráma miotail in uiscí níos doimhne. I bhfeirmacha iasc sliogánach an lae inniu fástar i málaí iad, agus is mór an éascaíocht é sin.

Fástar dhá chineál oisre in Éirinn faoi láthair. Tá an t-oisre dúchas Eorpach (Ostrea edulis) leibhéalta agus bíonn a shéasúr féin aige. Sceitheann sé le linn míonna an tsamhraidh, agus is i rith na míonna ina bhfuil litir 'r' i mBéarla is ceart é a ithe. Tosaíodh ag fás an chineáil eile—oisre an Chiúin-Aigéin (Crassotrea gigas)—in Éirinn sna 1970daí, le go mbeadh oisrí le fail sa tír i rith na bliana go léir. Tugtar 'cupán cloiche' nó gigas ar an gcineál seo freisin. Ní sceitheann siad i bhfarraigí na h Éireann mar go bhfuil an t-uisce ró-fhuar dóibh, ach sceitheann siad i ngorlanna agus bíonn fail orthu i rith na bliana.

Bíonn an t-oisre dúchais suas le cúig bliana de ghnáth sula mbíonn sé réidh le piocadh, ach ní thógann sé ach 18–28 mí ar oisrí an Chiúin-Aigéin fás chomh mór sin. Fástar iad seo ar fheirmeacha ag leibhéal an lag trá, agus fásann siad i bhfad níos dlúithe le chéile ná an cineál dúchais. Veigeatóirí iad na hoisrí, cosúil le ba nó le caoirigh; athraíonn siad plandaí in bhfeoil. Ach tá na plandaí a itheann na hoisrí chomh beag sin go gcaitear iad a scagadh isteach tríd na geolbhaigh. Ní chosnaíonn na plandaí ná an próiseas seo tada, rud a fhágann go bhfuil an t-oisre ina ainmhí an-fheiliúnach le fás ar fheirm sligéisc.

Tá oisrí ar an mbia sláinte is fearr dá bhfuil againn, mar go bhfuil siad ar bheagán calraí agus ar mhórán cothaithe. Tá go leor cailciam agus vitimíni A agus D iontu. Tá selenium agus sinc iontu agus tá an cháil orthu go bhfuil siad go maith chun torthúlachta. Cabhraíonn siad freisin le serotonin a chruthú, ábhar ceimiceach a chabhraíonn le codladh agus le goile. Cabhraíonn siad freisin le galrú a throid, agus is sláintiúla go mór mar chothú iad ná mórán de bhianna breise na linne seo.

Ceannach agus stóráil oisrí

Cé go bhféachann siad crua agus láidir, lobhann oisrí sách éasca. Ó tharla go mbíonn siad beo ar nós gach iasc sliogánach is furasta damáiste a dhéanamh dóibh nó iad a thruailliú, agus is ceart teocht ró-árd nó ró-íseal a sheachaint. *Nuair a bhíonn tú á gceannach, déan cinnte go mbíonn na sliogáin dúnta go docht, nó go dnúnann siad chomdh luath is a buailtear an buille beag is lú orthu. Ní ceart iad a chaitheamh anuas ar dhromchlaí crua, agus ní ceart go mbeadh na sliogáin briste.*

Nuair a bhíonn oisrí á stóráil ba cheart an sliogán leibhéalta a bheith in uachtar, le nach n-éalóidh an sú as an sliogán íochtair. Is ceart iad a phacáil go dlúth le chéile agus iad a stóráil ag teocht íseal in áit atá fionnuar, tais agus dorcha más féidir é; sin nó iad a chlúdach le héadach fliuch. Feileann íochtar an chuisneora go breá dóibh, agus ba cheart go mairfidís suas le seachtain ansin sa ngeimhreadh agus suas le ceithre lá sa samhradh

Oscailt oisrí

Féach ar na pictiúir (l. 19). Faigh scian oisrí nó ceann mar í. Cuir gob na scine isteach in inse an oisre agus sleamhnaigh an scian anuas trasna gar do bharr an tsliogáin, leis an matán a ghearradh. Scaoil an scian isteach faoin oisre ansin agus gearr an matán atá á cheangal den sliogán domhain. Beidh sé éasca ansin an bia a bhaint as an sliogán, le n-ithe nó le cócaráil

An raibh fhios agat?

Fásann péarlaí in oisrí. Bíonn líneáil de chruan lonrach ar an taobh istigh den sliogán, agus má théann gráinne gainimh nó a leithéid isteach ann clúdaíonn an t-oisre é le sraitheanna de néamhann péarlach, chun an fheoil a chosaint air. De réir mar a fhásann an t-oisre fásann an péarla timpeall an ghrainne. Ach ná bí ag súil le péarla i ngach oisre, mar ní tharlaíonn sé ach go hannamh, agus ní bhíonn ann ach péarla beag.

Wine and oysters

Martin Moran MW

The Bretons know a thing or two about raw oysters and wine. They wash the oysters down with Muscadet or the even more acidic local wine, Gros Plant. Burgundians will tell you, as will just about any food and wine guide, that Chablis is the classic choice. What these wines have in common is that they are bone dry, low on fruit and high on acidity and use no oak. They are, if you like, the vinous equivalent of a squirt of lemon.

There are plenty of others that will work just as well. Wines made from Sauvignon Blanc with its assertive, crisp dry character work particularly well. The Loire is France's best source with Sancerre or Pouilly Fumé the classic selections but Touraine and Quincy will cost less. Also in France, modern Bordeaux versions of the grape can be very good and relatively inexpensive.

Marlborough in New Zealand is now as classic a source for this grape as France and will provide plenty of star turns. Australia's best, most lemon like, come from the Adelaide Hills, Tasmania and Pemberton in Western Australia. South Africa too is rapidly becoming a source of first-rate Sauvignon, particularly in cool coastal areas like Constantia and Walker Bay. Chile has many examples of this grape but choose carefully as the best nearly all come from Casablanca.

Avoid the basic brands as they are simply too bland. Beware, too, oak-aged Sauvignons, which are very common in California.

The most lemony grape of all is probably Riesling, but it must be bone dry. Most examples from the Clare Valley are, but German Rieslings, even when designated as *trocken* or dry, still usually contain a little too much sweetness. Alsace is a better bet, especially from a top producer like Trimbach, renowned for the austerity of their Rieslings. Staying in Alsace, many Pinot Blancs should be fine and affordable too but Pinot Gris tends to be a little too lush and soft. Further afield Pinot Gris from Oregon or New Zealand can be drier and firmer and when it pops up in Northern Italy as Pinot Grigio it makes a less fruity and very dry style, which can work well.

White wines in Spain, Portugal and Greece have improved out of all recognition in recent years but the classic Iberian choice for any shellfish is an ice-cold Manzanilla Sherry. Elsewhere, the crisp dry whites from Rueda made by using local variety Verdejo either on its own or blended with Sauvignon Blanc are an excellent choice. Even better, though, might be the citrus-scented wines of the Albariño grape from Rias Baixas in Galicia. Across the border in Northern Portugal the choice would be a dry estate-bottled Vinho Verde, but not one of the medium-dry big brands. Greece has terrific native varieties but Retsina is not the best choice, rather a grape called Assyrtiko from the island of Santorini.

One of my favourite choices has to be a young Australian Hunter Semillon with its light citrus flavours, which is the ultimate wine partner should you be sitting at the edge of Sydney Harbour while consuming your oysters.

Champagne is the one wine everybody knows goes well with oysters, and so it does but certain styles work best. Blanc de Blanc, i.e. made only from Chardonnay, will have more of a lemon-like edge then most Champagnes, which are made using a blend of white and red varieties. Curiously, although wines may be labelled as Brut they can often be less than dry. The driest, and therefore the best choice, are those designated Brut Nature, Brut Sauvage or Ultra Brut.

Once you start cooking with oysters the choices change. If they are smoked, a not too fruity white made using oak is the answer and oak-aged white Rioja is the perfect partner. Dry rosés have freshness and a bit more body and flavour than whites so they are a great all-purpose choice for cooked oysters. Look for Clairets from Bordeaux, and Grenache-based wines from Navarra in Spain or Provence and the Southern Rhône.

Cream-based dishes such as chowders and some stews or pies have an affinity with Chardonnay and white Burgundies are the choice here. Alternatively, the more expensive, barrel-fermented and therefore less blatantly fruity, New World Chardonnays work well too.

If you must drink red make it as low on tannin as possible, so Beaujolais would be the choice, perhaps a Fleurie. Richer savoury dishes would probably work with Pinot Noir-based wines such as red Burgundy.

Finally, some critics say it is possible to drink any wine with any food provided you tweak the seasoning on the food. Tannic reds like a Barolo or young Bordeaux will taste metallic with raw oysters. However, sprinkle the oysters with salt or soy and a dash of lemon and expect a transformation that allows you to drink your favourite heavy red.

Soups

Oyster soup

Serves 6

18–24 oysters, shells removed, juices strained
 and reserved
2 large potatoes
110 g/4 oz pork belly, finely diced

600 ml/20 fl oz milk
bouquet garni
salt, freshly ground black pepper
40 g/1½ oz butter, cubed

Method

Fry the pork belly until crisp and set aside. Boil, peel and mash the potatoes. Heat the milk and add it to the mashed potatoes. Add the bouquet garni, salt and pepper and bring to the boil. Add the pork, oysters and juices and simmer gently for 2–3 minutes. Add the butter and mix gently. Check the seasoning and serve hot.

Note: you can use less milk if you prefer a thicker soup.

Galway Bay oyster bisque

Serves 4

12 Galway Bay oysters, chopped if large,
    juices reserved
3 tablespoons butter, melted
4 tablespoons white wine
25 g/1 oz onion, chopped
25 g/1 oz celery, chopped
25 g/1 oz cornflour or plain flour
25 g/1 oz button mushrooms, chopped

110 g/4 oz prawns or shrimps, cooked and shelled
3 dashes of Tabasco
1–2 drops of Worcestershire sauce
425 ml/15 fl oz milk plus reserved oyster juice
300 ml/10 fl oz double cream
Garnish
6 additional oysters, shells removed

Method
Place all the ingredients except the oysters, the milk/oyster juice mixture and the cream in a food processor. Add half the milk/oyster juice mixture and blend until smooth. Pour into a saucepan and cook with the rest of the milk/oyster juice for 6–8 minutes, whisking well. Mix in the cream and the chopped oysters and reheat very gently. Take care not to boil the bisque or the oyster meat will toughen.

To serve
Ladle into warm bowls and top with an oyster (you can leave the oysters raw or heat them for 1–2 minutes under the grill to plump them up).

Oyster and artichoke soup with carrageen moss

Serves 4

24 plump oysters, drained, chopped,
    juices strained and reserved
50 g/2 oz butter
50 g/2 oz scallions (green onions), chopped
1 garlic clove, crushed
50 g/2 oz mushrooms, finely chopped
1 x 500 g/16 oz can artichoke hearts,
    finely chopped
pinch of cayenne pepper

425 ml/15 fl oz fresh milk
3 g/1/8 oz carrageen moss, cleaned and tied loosely
    in muslin
50 ml/2 fl oz dry sherry or dry white wine
150 ml/5 fl oz cream
salt, freshly ground black pepper
Garnish
chopped parsley

Method

Melt the butter in a saucepan and gently sauté the scallions, garlic and mushrooms for 2–3 minutes. Add the artichoke hearts, parsley, cayenne pepper, milk, carrageen moss and oyster juices. Mix well and simmer gently until the soup thickens (10–15 minutes). Remove the carrageen bag, add the sherry and the oyster juices and bring the soup to boiling point. Remove the saucepan from the heat and blend the soup with a hand blender until smooth. Add the cream and oysters and reheat gently over a low heat until the oysters are heated through (about 3 minutes). Season to taste.

To serve

Serve in warm soup bowls or small demitasse cups garnished with parsley

Note: if you prefer a lighter soup omit the cream and add more milk.

Kilcornan oyster soup

This frothy broth is a delectable beginning to an elegant meal when served in demitasse cups.

Serves 4
12–18 oysters, shells removed,
    juices strained and reserved
225 ml/8 fl oz milk
225 ml/8 fl oz cream
25 g/1 oz butter

dash of Tabasco
salt, freshly ground black pepper
Garnishes
paprika
fingers of buttered toast

Method
Chop the oysters. Bring the milk, cream and butter to the boil in a saucepan, stirring continuously. Lower the heat slightly, add the chopped oysters, juices, Tabasco, salt and pepper and heat through.

To serve
Ladle the soup into warm soup bowls, sprinkle with a little paprika and serve at once with the toast.

Note: you can aerate the soup before adding the oysters by using a hand whisk. This will also make the soup more frothy.

Kilcornan House

Kilcornan House is a large 19th-century mansion near Clarinbridge. Now owned by a religious order, it was the home of the Redingtons, who were among the wealthiest landlords in County Galway. It typified the lifestyle of the Galway gentry. Each of its four floors had a distinctive use. The basement contained the kitchen, furnace and servants' workspaces. On the ground floor were rooms for entertainment, family rooms, library, games room and a chapel. Family bedrooms were on the first floor. The servants' quarters were on the top floor, from which there was a back stairs to the kitchen. The Redingtons were just and fair landlords, contributing immensely to the education and welfare of their tenants, and to the development of Clarinbridge village. Sir Thomas (1815–1862) was a Member of Parliament and held high positions in government.

Teach Chill Chornáin

Teach mór ón naoú céad déag é Teach Chill Chornáin in aice le Droichead an Chláirín. Is le ord rialta an teach anois, ach is anseo a bhí cónaí tráth ar na Redingtons, a bhí ar na tiarnaí talún ba shaibhre i gContae na Gaillimhe. Is sampla maith é do mhaithe agus uaisle na linne. Bhí cheithre urlár sa teach agus gach ceann aca le na fheidhm féin. Sa seomra íoslach a bhí an chistin, an fhoirnéis, agus ionad oibre na searbhóntaí. Ar an urlár talún bhí na seomraí fáilte agus féilte, seomraí clainne, leabharlann, seomra imeartha agus séipéal. Is ar an gcéad urlár a bhí seomraí leapan na clainne. Thuas i mbarr an tí a bhí seomraí na searbhóntaí, áit a raibh cúl-staighre go dtí an chistin. Ba tiarnaí talún cóir iad na Redingtons, a thug cothrom na féinne dá dtionóntaí agus tacaíocht do oideachas mhuintir na háite. Chuir siad go mór le forbairt Dhroichead an Chláirín. Bhí árd chéim ag Sir Thomas (1815–1862) sa Rialtas.

Kilcornan oyster soup

Kilcolgan oyster soup *(Oyster and mushroom soup)*

Serves 4

12–18 oysters, shells removed,
    juices strained and reserved
25 g/1 oz butter
225 g/8 oz onions, grated
2 medium potatoes, peeled and
    cut into small pieces
225 g/8 oz button mushrooms, chopped
225 ml/8 fl oz milk

225 ml/8 fl oz cream
dash of Tabasco
salt, freshly ground black pepper
Garnishes
paprika
fingers of hot buttered toast

Method

Melt the butter in a saucepan. Sauté the onions over a moderate heat until translucent.

Add the potatoes and mushrooms and sauté until tender. Pour in the milk and mix well. Add the cream and carefully bring to the boil, mixing gently.

Reduce the heat. Add the oysters, juices, Tabasco, salt and pepper and heat through (4–5 minutes).

To serve

Ladle the soup into warm soup bowls, sprinkle with a little paprika and serve at once with the toast.

Note: you can add a little dry white wine if the soup is too thick.

Maoilíosa's oyster bisque

Serves 4

12–18 oysters, shells removed,
    juices strained and reserved
1 large potato, peeled and cut into small cubes
2 teaspoons onion, finely chopped
1 tablespoon butter, melted
300 ml/10 fl oz milk
300 ml/10 fl oz cream
1 tablespoon parsley, chopped

celery salt or salt,
  freshly ground black pepper
Garnish
chopped parsley
Accompaniments
brown scones (see breads and scones)
pure Irish butter

Method

Place the oysters and juices in a saucepan and heat gently until the oysters are plump and curled at the edges. Drain, reserving the juices. Put the potato in a small saucepan, cover with water and bring to the boil. Reduce the heat and simmer until the potato is soft. Remove from the pan.

Sauté the onion in butter until it is translucent.

Put the cooked potato, milk, cream, onion, parsley, oyster juices and all but four of the oysters into a food processor. Blend until smooth.

Pour the bisque back into the saucepan, season to taste and warm over a gentle heat. Add the remaining four oysters.

To serve

Ladle the bisque into warm bowls, allowing one whole oyster per bowl, garnish with chopped parsley and serve with brown scones and butter.

Light dishes (cold)

Clarinbridge oysters

Clarinbridge oysters *(Oysters au naturel)*

Serves 4
24 Clarinbridge oysters
Garnishes
crushed ice and/or seaweed
1 lemon, cut into wedges

Accompaniments
Guinness bread (see breads and scones)
Guinness

Method
Scrub and rinse the oysters well. Open them carefully with an oyster knife—try not to spill the juices.

To serve
Cover a large platter with crushed ice or seaweed (or both). Carefully arrange the oysters and lemon wedges around the platter. Serve with Guinness bread and a glass of Guinness.

Thoor Ballylee

Thoor Ballylee oysters *(Oysters with cognac dressing)*

Serves 4

24 flat oysters in half shells
juice of 1 lemon
3 tablespoons cognac
salt, freshly ground black pepper

2 tablespoons olive oil
Garnishes
crushed ice
lettuce leaves

Method

Mix together the lemon juice, cognac, salt and pepper in a bowl. Add the olive oil very slowly, stirring continuously until the dressing is well combined.

To serve

Cover a large platter with crushed ice and arrange the lettuce leaves on top. Carefully arrange the oysters on top of the lettuce. Spoon the dressing over the oysters and serve.

Túr Bhaile Uí Lí

Cé gur le Contae Shligigh is mó a shamhlaítear W.B. Yeats, áit a bhfuil sé curtha, chaith sé blianta ina chónaí i seanteach túir a cheannaigh sé i mBaile Uí Lí, gar do áit chónaithe Lady Gregory. Chóirigh sé an túr, i bhfocail a dháin féin: 'With old mill boards and sea-green slates and smithy work from the Gort forge' agus bhaist sé Thoor Ballylee (Túr Bhaile Uí Lí) air. Anseo a chum sé roinnt de na dánta is fearr dá chuid. Is maith is fiú cuairt a thabhairt ar an túr mar tá amharc álainn ó bharr an túir ar thírdhreach dheisceart na Gaillimhe.

Thoor Ballylee

Among those who often visited the Gregory home was W.B. Yeats. While Yeats is associated very much with Sligo, where he is buried, he bought a derelict tower house near Coole at Ballylee. This he restored 'with old mill boards and sea-green slates, and smithy work from the Gort forge', then named it Thoor Ballylee—'*thoor*' being the Irish word for tower. It is worth a visit. When you have finished studying the Yeats memorabilia, you can have an expansive view of the south Galway countryside from the tower rooftop.

Yeats oysters *(Oysters with caviar)*

Serves 4
24 flat oysters in half shells with juices
2–3 teaspoons black caviar

Garnishes
crushed ice
1 lemon, cut into wedges

To serve
Cover a large platter with crushed ice. Carefully arrange the oysters around the platter and decorate with the lemon wedges. Top each oyster with caviar. Serve with chilled white wine or Champagne.

Note: you can use salmon roe instead of caviar.

Aran oysters *(Oysters with sausages)*

Cold raw oysters and sizzling hot sausages complement each other very well—give it a try and see!

Serves 4
24 cupped oysters in half-shells with juices
24 cocktail sausages
Sauce
150 ml/5 fl oz mayonnaise (see recipe page 42)

1 teaspoon horseradish sauce
2–3 tablespoons tomato ketchup
dash of Tabasco
dash of Worcestershire sauce

Method
Combine all of the sauce ingredients in a bowl and mix well. Pour the sauce into a small ramekin dish or bowl. Fry or grill the cocktail sausages until they are brown and crisp (8–10 minutes).

To serve
Place the sauce dish in the centre of a large platter and arrange the hot cocktail sausages around it. Insert some cocktail sticks into the sausages. Place the cold oysters, in their shells, around the sausages and serve.

James's oysters *(Oyster canapés)*

Serves 4

12 oysters, shells removed
75 g/3 oz butter

½ teaspoon mustard
12 circles brown or white toast
6 tablespoons mayonnaise (see recipe page 42)

Method

Mix the butter with ¼ teaspoon of mustard and spread on the circles of toast.
Place an oyster on each circle. Mix the mayonnaise with the remaining mustard and spoon over the oysters.

Note: you can use brown or cheese scones instead of toast if preferred.

Ardbear oysters *(Oysters with parsley topping)*

Serves 4

24 oysters in half shells
25 g/1 oz parsley, finely chopped
3–4 scallions (green onions), finely chopped
1 celery stalk, finely chopped
2 tablespoons mayonnaise (see recipe page 42)

1 tablespoon creamed horseradish sauce
2 tablespoons lemon juice
1 teaspoon wholegrain mustard
Accompaniments
sea vegetable muffins (see recipe page 120)
pure Irish butter

Method

Place the oysters on a serving platter. Blend the remaining ingredients in a food processor until smooth.
Spoon a little of the sauce over each oyster and serve with buttered sea vegetable muffins.

Quick mayonnaise

2 egg yolks
300 ml/½ pint olive oil

juice of 1 lemon (1 teaspoon approx)
salt and white pepper

Method
Put the egg yolks and salt in a blender. Blend a little and with the motor still running, very slowly pour in the oil until you get the correct consistency. (As the mayonnaise thickens the oil can be added a little faster.) Add the lemon juice and season to taste.

Ardfry House

Ardfry oysters *(Oyster cocktail)*

Serves 4

16–20 oysters in half shells,
    juices strained and reserved

Sauce
3–4 tablespoons mayonnaise (see recipe above)
2 tablespoons tomato ketchup
1 tablespoon horseradish, grated
dash of lemon juice
dash of Worcestershire sauce

dash of Tabasco

Garnishes
chopped parsley or paprika
lettuce leaves

Accompaniments
white kombu crisps bread (see page 117)
pure Irish butter

Method

Mix all the sauce ingredients and the oyster juices together in a bowl. Remove the oysters from their shells and set aside. Spoon a little of the sauce into each clean, empty shell. Lay an oyster on top and spoon over some more sauce.

To serve

Sprinkle with parsley or paprika. Place the oysters on a bed of lettuce on four starter plates. Serve with the bread and butter.

Aird Fhraoigh

Anseo in Aird Fhraoigh ar Chuan na Gaillimhe, gar don áit a bhfuil an Galway Bay Golf and Country Club anois, a bhí an chéad stáisiún oifigiúil taighde sligéisc in Éirinn. Bhí ainm an-ardnósach air: 'The Ardfry Experimental Oyster Cultivation Station', *agus tá tagairt ag N. Wilkins dó ina leabhar* Squires, Spalpeens and Sprats *lth. 45. Ní haon ionadh, mar sin, gur roghnaíodh Aird Fhraoigh arís mar láthair don Institiúid Mhuirí (Marine Institute), an áisíneacht náisiúnta taighde mara, a haistríodh as Baile Átha Cliath go cósta an iarthair tamall ó shin.*

Ardfry

Ardfry, near the Galway Bay Golf and Country Club, was the site for Ireland's first shellfish research station. The authorities referred to it as 'The Ardfry Experimental Oyster Cultivation Station', although Noël Wilkins thought this a rather grandiose title for what was a relatively simple facility (see Noël Wilkins, *Squires, Spalpeens and Sprats* p.45). Ardfry is now the location for the Marine Institute, the national marine research agency, recently transferred from Dublin.

Oisrí Liam

Oisrí Liam *(Oysters with smoked salmon)*

Serves 4
24 oysters in half shells
2 slices smoked salmon
2–3 tablespoons mayonnaise (see recipe above)
1 teaspoon lemon juice

Garnishes
4–8 small strips of smoked salmon
1 tablespoon chives, chopped
Accompaniments
quick dulse brown bread (see page 119)
pure Irish butter

Method
Blend the salmon, mayonnaise and lemon juice in a food processor until smooth. Spoon the salmon mixture over the oysters.

To serve
Garnish with the salmon strips and chives and serve with buttered dulse bread.

Smoked oyster and egg canapés

Serves 4
24 smoked oysters, vacuum packed or in brine
4 eggs
salt, freshly ground black pepper
15 g/½ oz butter
2 tablespoons mayonnaise (see page 42)

2 tablespoons chopped chives
fronds of dill
Accompaniments
12 brown scones (see page 122)
pure Irish butter

Method
Beat the eggs in a bowl with salt and pepper. Melt the butter in a saucepan, add the egg and cook very gently until creamy, mixing continuously. Set aside to cool. When the egg mixture is cool, add the mayonnaise and chives and mix well.

To serve
Cut the scones in half, butter them and place them on a large platter. Spoon the egg mixture on to the scones and top each one with a smoked oyster and some dill.

Deirdre's oysters *(Oyster and spinach salad)*

Serves 4

24 oysters, shells removed and juices reserved
75 g/3 oz bacon rashers, diced
1 medium red pepper, cut into fine strips
2 tablespoons wine vinegar

3 tablespoons sunflower oil
freshly ground black pepper
1 bunch fresh young spinach leaves, washed and dried

Method

Fry the bacon until crisp, remove and drain on kitchen paper. Fry the pepper strips to soften a little, then remove them and drain. Add the wine vinegar, oil and oyster juice to the pan and bring to the boil to reduce a little. Return the peppers and bacon to the pan and add the oysters. Reheat quickly, just to warm the oysters through. Season to taste.

To serve

Arrange the spinach leaves on four plates. Spoon the oysters over the spinach and drizzle the warm dressing over them.

Oyster shot

Serves 1

1 oyster
1½ teaspoons vodka
4 tablespoons tomato juice

1 tablespoon lime juice
3 drops Worcestershire sauce
1 drop Tabasco

Method

Mix all the ingredients except the oyster in a shot glass. Drop in a fresh, raw oyster before serving.

Dooras House oysters *(Oyster salad)*

Serves 4

12–16 oysters, shells removed
    (4 shell halves retained)
2 tablespoons sunflower oil
Dressing
1 teaspoon lemon juice
1 garlic clove, peeled and crushed
2 tablespoons olive oil
salt, freshly ground black pepper

Coating
1 tablespoon fine breadcrumbs
1 tablespoon Parmesan cheese, freshly
    grated
1 tablespoon parsley, chopped
freshly ground black pepper
Garnishes
1 small red onion, finely grated
1 tablespoon of red wine vinegar
selection of lettuce leaves

Method

Mix all the dressing ingredients in a bowl until well combined. Set aside.

Mix the breadcrumbs, Parmesan, parsley and pepper together in a bowl. Toss the oysters in the crumb mixture and chill for half an hour to allow the oysters to firm up and the coating to settle. Pour the oil into a frying pan and, when hot, fry the oysters until golden all over.

Mix together the red onion and red wine vinegar.

To serve

In a large bowl, toss the lettuce leaves in the dressing. Arrange the oysters on top. Spoon the red onion mixture into the oyster shells and serve alongside the salad.

Light dishes (warm)

James's oyster and salmon sausage with mustard cream sauce

For the past few years I have had the pleasure of being a judge at the Associated Craft Butchers of Ireland competition for speciality sausages and this triggered the idea of an oyster–salmon sausage.

Serves 4

8 plump oysters, shells removed
225 g/8 oz fresh Irish salmon
4 tablespoons fresh double cream
1 large egg white
dash of Tabasco
pinch of salt
cayenne pepper

Mustard cream sauce

225 ml/8 fl oz cream
60 ml/2 fl oz dry white wine
1 tablespoon Lakeshore Guinness mustard (or other mustard of your choice)
1 teaspoon (approx.) lemon juice
salt, freshly ground black pepper

Method

Put all the oyster sausage ingredients in a food processor and blend until smooth. Place two teaspoonfuls of the mixture on a strip of cling film about 10 cm/4 in wide. Roll the mixture in the cling film to form a sausage approximately 7 cm/3 in long. Twist the ends tightly to secure the sausage and maintain its shape. Wrap a piece of tinfoil tightly around the sausage. Repeat this process with the remaining mixture (you should get 4–6 sausages).

Place the sausages in a wide, flat saucepan of simmering water and simmer gently for 5–6 minutes. When the sausages are cooked, remove them from the saucepan and unwrap them carefully.

Make the sauce while the sausages are cooking. Pour the cream and wine into a saucepan, add the mustard and stir continuously over a low heat until the mixture reduces and the sauce has a nice thick consistency. Flavour with the lemon juice and seasoning.

To serve

Pour the mustard sauce over the oyster-salmon sausages and serve hot.

Note: a pinch of finely chopped parsley or basil leaves may be added to the sausage mixture for variety and colour.

Celebration oysters *(Oysters with Pernod)*

Serves 4

24 cupped oysters in half shells with juices
25 g/1 oz butter
225 g/8 oz spinach, washed and torn
25 g/1 oz parsley, chopped
1 tablespoon Worcestershire sauce
¼ teaspoon Tabasco

1 teaspoon anchovy paste
2 tablespoons Pernod
4 tablespoons grated Parmesan or Gubbeen cheese
Accompaniments
white kombu crisps bread (see page 117)
pure Irish butter

Method

Melt the butter in a saucepan. Add the spinach, parsley, Worcestershire sauce, Tabasco, anchovy paste and Pernod. Stir over a low heat until the spinach has wilted. Pour the mixture into a food processor and blend until it is well combined.

Preheat the grill to high. Place the oysters on a baking tray, being careful not to spill the juices. Flash under the grill for a few seconds until the edges of the oysters curl. Remove the baking tray from the grill and reduce the heat slightly.

Cover the oysters with the sauce and sprinkle with grated cheese. Grill until the oysters are heated through and the tops are golden (6–8 minutes).

To serve

Serve with thick slices of the kombu crisps bread and plenty of butter.

Note: crushed tinfoil on the baking tray will keep the oysters steady while cooking.

Connemara oysters with boxty

Connemara oysters *(Oysters with boxty)*

A wonderful contrast of succulent oysters with golden potato boxty. The humble Irish potato is transformed into a sophisticated starter or light lunch, worthy to be served with oysters and cream.

Serves 4

12–16 cupped oysters, shells removed

Boxty

2 large potatoes, peeled

25 g/1 oz plain flour

1 egg, beaten (optional)

pinch of salt

sunflower oil and butter for frying

Garnish

sour cream

Method

Coarsely grate the potatoes into a bowl, season with salt and add the flour. Mix thoroughly. Heat the oil and butter in a heavy frying pan over moderate heat. Fry the potatoes in spoonfuls, turning until golden on both sides.

Toss the oysters in the hot pan for about a minute to firm them.

To serve

Place the boxty on warm plates, add a dollop of sour cream and top with the warmed oysters.

Note: the egg makes the boxty lighter and also adds to the food value, but boxty without egg is more traditional.

Coole oysters *(Roasted oysters with fennel)*

This dish is perfect for a barbecue.

Serves 4

24 oysters, unopened

1–2 tablespoons green fennel leaves, finely chopped

110 g/4 oz butter, melted

salt, freshly ground black pepper

Garnishes

8 lemon wedges

Accompaniments

quick cheese bread (see page 119)

pure Irish butter

Method

Preheat the oven to 220°C/425°F/gas mark 7. Scrub and wash the oysters. Roast them on a baking tray in the oven until the shells open (3–4 minutes). Remove the top shell. Mix the fennel leaves with the warm melted butter, season with salt and pepper and spoon over the oysters.

To serve

Serve with lemon wedges, cheese bread and butter.

Irwin's oysters *(Oysters Florentine)*

Serves 4

24 cupped oysters, shells removed and retained
90 ml/3 fl oz mornay sauce (see recipe below)
50 g/2 oz butter
225 g/8 oz spinach, washed and torn
salt, fresh ground black pepper

Garnish
paprika
Accompaniment
sea vegetable muffins (see page 120)

Method
Make the mornay sauce and keep warm.
Melt the butter in a saucepan and sauté the spinach until it wilts. Season to taste.
Preheat the grill to high. Place the oyster shells on a baking tray. Cover each shell with a layer of buttered spinach. Place an oyster on top and spoon some mornay sauce over each one.
Grill the oysters until the tops are glazed and golden (8–10 minutes).

To serve
Sprinkle with a little paprika and serve with sea vegetable muffins

Note: crushed tinfoil on the baking tray will keep the oysters steady while cooking.

Mornay sauce

50 g/2 oz butter
25 g/1 oz plain flour
pinch of salt

300 ml/½ pint milk
2 teaspoons fresh cream
75 g/3 oz Irish farmhouse cheese, grated

Method
Put all the ingredients in a saucepan, place over a medium heat and using a balloon whisk, keep whisking until the sauce is cooked and thickened. This works for me always and is a very fast method.

Note: if you want a very rich mornay sauce, whisk in 1 egg yolk with the cream. This is a good glazing sauce for grilled oysters.

Gambler's oysters (Las Vegas oysters)

Serves 4

24 cupped oysters in half shells with juices
6 bacon rashers, rinds removed
25 g/1 oz butter
1 large onion, finely chopped
½ medium green pepper, deseeded and
      finely chopped

1–2 garlic cloves, minced
2 tablespoons parsley, chopped
1 teaspoon anchovy paste
dash of Tabasco
salt, freshly ground black pepper

Method

Preheat the grill to high. Partially cook the bacon under the grill for about 2 minutes on each side. Remove from the grill, maintaining the temperature.

Melt the butter in a saucepan and sauté the onion, pepper, garlic and parsley for about 2 minutes. Add the anchovy paste, Tabasco, salt and pepper and continue to sauté until the vegetables are soft.

Place the oysters on the baking tray, taking care not to spill the juices. Put a teaspoonful of filling on each oyster and top with a piece of partially cooked bacon. Place under the grill and cook until the bacon is crisp (3–4 minutes).

Note: crushed tinfoil on the baking tray will keep the oysters steady while cooking.

Oysters Benedict

Serves 4

8 oysters, shells removed
25 g/1 oz butter
4 thin slices of ham, cut to fit muffins
4 poached eggs (kept warm)

2 English muffins, halved, toasted and buttered
1 recipe Hollandaise sauce (see recipe below)
Garnish
chopped parsley

Method

Melt the butter in a saucepan and sauté the ham for about 2 minutes, just to warm it. Remove from the pan. In the same pan, sauté the oysters until the edges begin to curl (2–3 minutes). Poach the eggs and toast and butter the halved muffins. Place the ham on the muffin halves and top with a poached egg. Cover the egg with 1–2 tablespoons of Hollandaise sauce. Place two oysters on top of each egg.

To serve

Garnish with parsley and serve immediately.

Hollandaise sauce

3 tablespoons white wine vinegar
6–8 peppercorns
1 blade mace
1 bay leaf

4 egg yolks
pinch of salt
110 g/4oz butter, melted
lemon juice

Method

Place the vinegar, peppercorns, mace and bay leaf in a saucepan and simmer over a low heat until reduced to one-third. Strain. Put the egg yolks, reduced vinegar mixture and salt into a liquidiser.
While the motor is running, add the melted butter in a slow stream. Finally, add lemon juice to taste. Pour into a warm jug and stand in a bowl of hot water to keep the sauce warm.

Oranmore oysters *(Savoury oyster rolls)*

A snack suitable for the traveller who passes through this vibrant village, which lies
eight kilometres east of Galway city.

Serves 4

16–24 cupped oysters, shells removed,
   juices strained and reserved
4 small bread rolls
110 g/4 oz butter, melted

150 ml/5 fl oz fresh cream
150 ml/5 fl oz sour cream
freshly ground black pepper

Method
Preheat the oven to 200°C/400°F/gas mark 6. Cut the bread rolls in two and scoop out some of the soft centre. Brush the insides of the rolls with the melted butter and crisp in the oven until golden (3–5 minutes). Pour the reserved oyster juices into a saucepan over moderate heat. Add the fresh cream and sour cream, raise the temperature and whisk until the sauce thickens. Add the oysters and warm through (about 3 minutes). Sprinkle with pepper.

To serve
Spoon the oysters and sauce on to the crispy bread rolls and serve immediately.

Brian Martyn oysters *(Barbecued oysters)*

Serves 4
16–24 oysters in half shells with juices
2 tablespoons fresh lemon or lime juice
2 tablespoons soy sauce
¼ teaspoon garlic, crushed
¼ teaspoon ginger, grated
¼ teaspoon hot chilli powder
1 teaspoon sesame oil

Garnish
lemon wedges
Accompaniments
quick Guinness bread (see page 118)
pure Irish butter

Method
Preheat a barbecue or grill to high. Mix all the ingredients except the oysters until well combined. Place the oysters carefully on the barbecue or grill. Spoon some sauce over each one and cook for 6–8 minutes until sizzling.

To serve
Serve the oysters hot on a large platter with Guinness bread, butter and lemon wedges.

Note: you can also put the oysters on the barbecue unopened. Cook until they open, remove the top shell and spoon the sauce over them.

The Martyns

The Galway Martyns were a formidable lot. They included merchants, landowners, politicians, lawyers, soldiers, duellists and scholars. A noteworthy member of the Tullira Martyns was Edward (1859–1923). A large landowner, with an Oxford education, he nevertheless spoke and wrote fluently in Irish and played a central role in the Irish Theatre and Celtic Revival Movement. One of the current Martyns is Brian, a producer of some of the finest oysters in south Galway.

Na Máirtínigh

Bhain Máirtínigh na Gaillimhe cáil mhór amach dóibh féin mar thrádálaithe, úinéirí talún, polaiteoirí, dlíodóirí, saighdiúirí, scoláirí agus lucht comhraic aonair. Ba duine de Mháirtínigh Thul Oidhre é Edward Martyn (1859–1923), fear a fuair a chuid oideachais in Oxford, a raibh réimse mór talún ina sheilbh, agus a raibh labhairt agus scríobh na Gaeilge ar a thoil aige. Bhí sé rannpháirteach sa Celtic Revival Movement agus bhí ról lárnach aige i mbunú Amharclann na Mainisteach, in éineacht le Yeats agus Lady Gregory.
Is duine de Mháirtínigh an lae inniu i nGaillimh, Brian Martyn, tairgeoir oisrí.

Grilled oysters with wine and cheese sauce

Serves 4

24 oysters in half shells, juices
    strained and reserved
15 g/½ oz butter
1 tablespoon plain flour

150 ml/5 fl oz white wine
50 g/2 oz grated Cheddar or Parmesan cheese
extra grated cheese for topping

Method

Melt the butter in a saucepan over a low heat. Add the flour and mix vigorously. Add the wine and oyster juices slowly, whisking continuously. Add the cheese and continue whisking until the sauce is thick and creamy. Remove from the heat.

Preheat the grill to high. Place the oysters on a baking tray, spoon a little sauce over each oyster and sprinkle with the extra cheese. Place under the grill and cook for 5–6 minutes until the cheese is golden brown and sizzling. Serve immediately.

Ballybrit oyster soufflés

Serves 4

12 oysters, shells removed, finely chopped
butter for greasing
50 g/2 oz Parmesan
3 small eggs, separated

210 ml/7 fl oz béchamel sauce (see recipe page 61)
salt, freshly ground black pepper
Garnish
fingers of hot buttered toast or brown bread (see
    page 120)

Method

Preheat the oven to 180°C/350°F/gas mark 4. Grease four individual soufflé/ramekin dishes with butter and dust with a little of the cheese.

Whisk the egg yolks into the hot béchamel sauce off the heat. Add the remaining cheese and season with salt and pepper.

In a very clean bowl, whisk the egg whites with a pinch of salt until stiff. Add a little of the egg white and the oysters to the cheese mixture and mix well. Very gently fold in the remaining egg whites. Divide the soufflé mixture amongst the dishes and bake for about 15 minutes until firm and brown on top.

To serve

Serve the soufflés straight from the oven with fingers of toast or brown bread, accompanied by a glass of chilled white wine.

Ballybrit oyster soufflés

Béchamel sauce

300 ml/½ pint milk
1 medium onion, peeled
1 bay leaf

5–6 white peppercorns
25g/1 oz butter
25g/1 oz plain flour
pinch of salt

Method
Pour the milk into a saucepan, add the onion, bay leaf and peppercorns and simmer over a very low heat for 5–10 minutes until the flavours infuse. Strain the milk into a jug or bowl discarding the peppercorns, onion and bay leaf.
Put the milk and the remaining ingredients into a saucepan, place over a medium heat and using a balloon whisk, keep whisking until the sauce is cooked and thickened.

Ballybrit

Is there anybody who has not been to, or at least heard about, the Galway Races? Highlight of the calendar in the city is the week-long racing festival in late July/ early August. Punters (with more stamina than the horses) start their vacation with Race Week and round off their western holidays with a canter to an Oyster Festival later.

Baile an Bhriota

Cá bhfuil an té nár chuala caint ar Rásaí na Gaillimhe, ar ráschúrsa Bhaile an Bhriota ar imeall thoir chathair na Gaillimhe? Ní bréag ar bith mardi gras *na Gaillimhe a thabhairt ar an tseachtain rásaí capall seo, ag deireadh Mhí Iúil agus tús Mhí Lúnasa gach bliain. Le blianta beaga anuas, roghnaíonn go leor daoine an tráth seo bliana i gcomhair a gcuid laethanta saoire, chun freastal ar dhá ócáid ar leith: Rásaí na Gaillimhe agus Féile na nOisrí.*

Corrib crêpes *(Oyster and spinach crêpes)*

Serves 4
24 oysters, shells removed,
    juices strained and reserved
1 recipe pancake/crêpe mixture (see below)
1 recipe cheese sauce (see below)

25 g/1 oz butter
1 teaspoon chopped scallions (green onions)
225 g/8 oz spinach, washed and torn
extra cheese for sprinkling

Method
Preheat the oven to 180°C/350°F/gas mark 4. Grease a medium-sized ovenproof dish.
Make the crêpes. Make the cheese sauce and keep it warm.
Melt the butter in a saucepan and sauté the scallions for 2–3 minutes. Add the spinach and sauté until it wilts. Poach the oysters in their own juices for 1–2 minutes and then chop them coarsely. Place the oysters in a large bowl and add the spinach and scallions. Fold in half of the warm cheese sauce and mix gently.
Place 2–3 tablespoons of the oyster mixture in the centre of each crêpe and roll up firmly. Place the filled crêpes side by side in the ovenproof dish. Cover with the remaining cheese sauce and sprinkle the extra cheese on top. Bake for 10–15 minutes until golden brown and bubbling.

To serve
Serve the hot crêpes with chilled white wine.

Pancakes/Crêpes

110 g/4 oz self-raising flour
pinch of salt
1 small egg

1 teaspoon oil or melted butter
300 ml/10 fl oz milk
sunflower oil or butter

Method
Sieve the flour and salt into a bowl. Make a well in the centre, drop in the egg and add the oil or melted butter and some of the milk. Whisk until very smooth. Add the rest of the milk and whisk until you have a nice smooth batter. Place a small knob of butter or some sunflower oil on a hot crêpe pan. Pour two tablespoons of batter into the hot pan, making sure the whole surface is covered. Cook quickly for 1–2 minutes until golden and then turn over and cook on the other side. Keep the pancakes/crêpes warm until ready to serve.

Note: if you are not using your batter immediately, cover and store it in the fridge or in a cool place until needed.

Cheese sauce

25 g/1 oz butter
25 g/1 oz plain flour
pinch of salt

300 ml/½ pint milk
75 g/3 oz Irish farmhouse cheese, grated

Method
Put all the ingredients in a saucepan, place over a medium heat and whisk with a balloon whisk, whisking until the sauce is cooked and thickened. This works for me always and is a very fast method.
Note: try some of the good Irish farmhouse cheeses now available—Gubbeen, Gabriel etc.

Jamie's oysters

Serves 4
12 oysters in half shells with juices
2 shallots, finely chopped
1 tablespoon butter, melted

2 tablespoons white wine
110 g/4 oz butter
3 teaspoons lemon juice
salt, freshly ground black pepper

Method
Preheat the grill to high. Flash the oysters for a few seconds under the grill until plump and curled at the edges. Drain, retaining the juices, and keep warm.
Sauté the shallots in the melted butter for 2–3 minutes. Add the wine and strained oyster juices and stir over a medium heat until the liquid reduces to about 3 tablespoons. Add the solid butter, bit by bit, whisking constantly to thicken the sauce. Add the lemon juice, salt and pepper.

To serve
Spoon the sauce over the warm oysters and serve immediately.

Diarmuid's oysters *(Oyster and potato blinis)*

Serves 4

12 oysters, shells removed
1–2 large potatoes, peeled
        and chopped into small pieces
2 medium eggs

salt
oil and butter for frying
Garnish
sour cream

Method

Put the potatoes, egg and salt in a food processor and blend until smooth. Heat the butter and oil in a heavy frying pan and fry spoonfuls of the potato mixture until golden on both sides. The mixture should yield around 12 blinis.

To serve

Place a dollop of sour cream on each blini and top with the raw oysters.

Note: smoked oysters are also good with blinis.

Máire's oysters *(Oysters with wild rice)*

Serves 4

24 large cupped oysters in half shells, juices
        strained and reserved
60 ml/2 fl oz dry sherry
1 tablespoon lemon juice
225 g/8 oz wild rice
50 g/2 oz butter

½ medium green pepper, deseeded & finely chopped
225 g/8 oz mushrooms, finely chopped
1–2 tablespoons parsley, chopped
dash of Tabasco
salt, freshly ground black pepper

Method

Cook the wild rice according to the instructions on the packet. Once the rice is cooked, place it in an ovenproof dish and dry in the oven at 180°C/350°F/gas mark 4 for a few minutes.
Melt the butter in a saucepan and sauté the pepper, mushrooms and parsley until tender. Add the Tabasco and a little salt and pepper. Add the vegetable mixture to the wild rice and mix well.
Preheat the oven to 200°C/400°F/gas mark 6. Place the oysters on a baking tray. Spoon some of the rice mixture on to each oyster. Mix the oyster juices, sherry and lemon juice in a bowl and spoon a little of this mixture over each oyster. Bake until the oysters are heated right through (7–10 minutes).

To serve

Serve with a bottle of your favourite Champagne.

Kylemore oyster breakfast *(Scrambled eggs with oysters and smoked salmon)*

Serves 2–4

8–12 oysters, juices strained and oysters chopped
30 ml/2 tablespoons milk or cream
50 g/2 oz butter
salt, freshly ground black pepper
4–6 large eggs, beaten

Garnishes
4–8 slices of Irish smoked salmon
4–8 additional oysters in half shells (optional)
Accompaniments
quick dulse brown bread (see breads and scones)
pure Irish butter

Method

Mix the milk/cream, butter and seasoning in a non-stick saucepan. Bring to the boil and pour in the eggs and oysters and mix gently until the mixture is creamy. Don't have the heat too high or both the eggs and the oysters will be tough. Take the saucepan off the heat before the eggs are fully cooked and keep mixing. The heat of the saucepan is enough to finish the cooking.

To serve

Serve the scrambled eggs and oysters on top of a slice or two of Irish smoked salmon with a few extra oysters on the side. Enjoy this Irish breakfast with dulse bread and butter.

Kylemore Castle and Abbey

No visitor to Connemara leaves the area without calling to scenic Kylemore. The Castle was built by Mitchell and Margaret Henry in the 1860s. Included in the construction were two small churches, one a replica of Norwich Cathedral. Mitchell Henry was a good landlord which helped him to hold a seat in the House of Commons. The estate passed to a number of owners until taken over and renamed Kylemore Abbey by the Benedictine nuns of Ypres in 1920. For a time the nuns ran a plush guesthouse which was very popular with fishermen. They would have enjoyed this Irish breakfast with the free-range eggs, butter and cream from the Abbey farm, not to mention the bread from the bakery.

Caisleán agus Mainistir na Coille Móire

Ní fhágann an turasóir ceantar Chonamara gan cuairt ar an Choill Mhór. Tógadh an caisleán ag na Henrys ins na 1860s. Tógadh dhá shéipéal ag an am céanna, ceann aca mac samhail do Árd Theampall Norwich. Ba tiarna talún cineálta Mitchell Henry rud a chabhraigh leis suiochán a fháil sa Pharlimint. Dathraí úinéaracht an tsealúchais go minic go dtí gur ghlac mná rialta Ypres ó ord Naomh Benedict seilbh air i 1920. Bhíodh teach aíochta aca a raibh cáil agus cliú air i measc iascairí. Nach iad a bhaineadh an sásamh as an mbricfeasta seo, le uibheacha, im agus uachtar ó fheirm na mainistreach gan trácht ar na aráin ón mbácús.

Clarinbridge oyster omelette

This is a very good brunch dish and makes excellent bar food.

Serves 1
5–6 Clarinbridge oysters, drained and chopped
1–2 bacon rashers
1 teaspoon double cream (optional)
salt, freshly ground black pepper

2 large eggs, beaten
Accompaniments
green salad
roast potato wedges or quick dulse brown bread (see breads and scones)

Method
Fry the rashers in a frying pan until crisp. Remove the rashers from the pan, retaining the fat, and crumble them. Fry the oysters in the bacon fat for 1–2 minutes, then add the crumbled bacon. Mix well and remove from the heat. Add the cream and seasoning to the eggs and mix well. Cook the egg mixture in a hot, non-stick omelette pan until just set, incorporating as many folds as possible while cooking. Place the oyster and rasher mixture in the centre and fold over.

To serve
Serve with salad and potato wedges or dulse bread.

Droichead an Chláirín

Sráidbhaile gleoite cois cósta é Droichead an Chláirín, suite ar an N18, 16 ciliméadar ó dheas de chathair na Gaillimhe. Tá oisrí á bhfás agus á saothrú le blianta fada, sna góilíní beaga mara ó thuaidh agus ó dheas den bhaile, agus is é an baile seo anois croílár oisrí na Gaillimhe. Ócáid mhór turasóireachta í Féile Oisrí Dhroichead an Chláirín gach bliain. Tagann daoine ó chian agus ó chóngar chuig an bhféile, agus tá an líon turasóirí ag dul i méid ó bhliain go bliain.

Clarinbridge

The seashore village of Clarinbridge, about 16 km from Galway city on the N18, is the nerve centre of Galway's oyster activity. For centuries oysters have been harvested in the numerous inlets to the north and south of the village. This heritage is celebrated by the annual Clarinbridge Oyster Festival which brings so many tourists, celebrities and locals together that there is just about enough elbow room to balance your plate of the molluscs and drink whatever you're having yourself.

Oyster pancakes

Serves 4

12 large oysters, chopped,
    juices strained and reserved
75 g/3 oz butter
1 leek, finely chopped
1 shallot, finely chopped
2 tablespoons plain flour
150 ml/5 fl oz white wine

150 ml/5 fl oz double cream or milk
1 tablespoon parsley, finely chopped
salt, freshly ground black pepper
8 warm pancakes (see page 62)
Garnishes
parsley
lemon wedges

Method

Melt the butter in a saucepan and sauté the leek and shallot until soft (5–8 minutes). Add the flour and mix thoroughly. Add the oyster juices, wine and cream/milk, mix well and cook for 4–5 minutes until the sauce has a creamy consistency. Add the oysters and heat gently. Add the parsley and season to taste.

To serve

Spread each pancake with the hot oyster mixture, roll up and place on a hot platter. Garnish with parsley and lemon wedges and serve immediately.

St Patrick's Day oysters *(Oysters with spinach and parsley sauce)*

Serves 4

12–18 oysters in half shells
Sauce
225 g/8 oz spinach, cooked and drained
50 g/2 oz butter, melted
1 tablespoon chives, finely chopped

2 tablespoons parsley, finely chopped
dash of Worcestershire sauce
dash of Tabasco
Topping
50 g/2 oz fine breadcrumbs
75 g/3 oz butter, melted

Method

Preheat the grill to high. Place the oysters on some crumpled tinfoil on a large baking tray and flash under the grill for 1–2 minutes or until the edges curl. Blend all the sauce ingredients in a food processor until smooth. Spoon the sauce over the warm oysters. Top with the buttered crumbs and grill until golden, about 4 minutes.

Oysters with Irish black pudding, honey and apple

Oyster potato soufflé

Serves 4

12 oysters, drained, chopped, juices reserved
225 g/8 oz potatoes
4 tablespoons double cream
1 large egg, beaten

50 g/2 oz butter, melted
salt, freshly ground black pepper
15 g/½ oz fine breadcrumbs

Method

Preheat the oven to 200ºC/400ºF/gas mark 6. Grease a soufflé dish (approx 18–20 cm/7–8 inches diameter). Boil, peel and finely mash the potatoes. Mix the cream, egg, half of the melted butter and the salt and pepper together. Add the potatoes and the chopped oysters and blend well. Spoon the mixture into the soufflé dish. Toss the breadcrumbs in the remaining butter and sprinkle over the top. Bake for 30–40 minutes until the top is golden.

Note: for a richer soufflé mixture, use two eggs instead of one. Separate them and mix the yolks with the cream and add to the potato mixture. Whisk the egg whites, with a tiny pinch of salt, to peak stage, then fold them gently into the potato mixture at the same time as the chopped oysters. For single servings use 4 individual ramekin dishes and bake for 15–20 minutes.

Oysters with Irish black pudding, honey and apple

Serves 4

4–8 oysters, drained, juices reserved
50 g/2 oz unsalted butter

4 slices black pudding
4 large slices eating apple, cored but not peeled
2 tablespoons Irish honey

Method

Melt half of the butter in a frying pan and fry the black pudding until crisp on both sides. Remove from the pan and wipe the pan clean. Fry the apple slices in a mixture of honey and the remaining butter until golden on both sides and tender but not soft. Remove the apple from the pan and keep warm. Fry the oysters until plump and heated through.

To serve

Place an apple slice on each of four warm starter plates. Place a slice of black pudding on top of the apple and top it off with the oysters. Dribble the honey butter from the pan around the plate and serve at once.

Note: you could serve the honey butter in a clean oyster shell instead of dribbling it on to the plates.

Oysters topped with goats' cheese

Serves 4

12–16 oysters in half shells
2–3 tablespoons pesto

8–12 rounds goats' cheese
Garnish
pinch of cayenne pepper

Method

Preheat the grill to high. Loosen the oysters from their lower hinge and settle them, in their shells, on a bed of crumpled tinfoil on a grill pan. Flash under the hot grill for a minute or two until the edges curl. Spoon a little pesto over each one and top with a flattened round of goats' cheese. Flash under the grill again until the cheese melts and begins to bubble.

To serve

Sprinkle with a tiny pinch of cayenne pepper and serve at once.

Oysters with truffles *(Huitres gratinées au sabayon de truffes)*

An inspiration from the music of Jean Michel Jarre.

Serves 1–22

6 cupped oysters, shells removed, juices strained
    and reserved.
110 g/4 oz fresh spinach, wilted in a little melted
    seasoned butter

Sauce
1 egg yolk
50 g/2 oz butter cut in small pieces
15 g/½ oz fine slivers of truffle

Method

Clean the oyster shells. Place a little of the spinach in each shell and top with an oyster. Spread some truffle on top. Place a heat-proof bowl over a saucepan of hot water, making sure the water doesn't touch the bottom of the bowl. Pour in the oyster juice, add the egg yolk and mix to a smooth emulsion.
Remove the bowl from the heat and add the butter, bit by bit, whisking continuously. When the sauce is a nice coating consistency, coat the oysters. Place under a hot grill and cook until golden—about 5–6 minutes.

To serve

Enjoy with a glass of Champagne.

Jean Michel Jarre

Díoltar furmhór do oisrí na h-Éireann sa bFhrainc. Dearbhaíonn sé seo má tá gá le dearbhú ar cháil na Fraince mar thír le cuisine don scoth; chomh maith leis an meas atá aca freisin arna h-ealaín i gcoitiana,agus na mindána in a n-iomlán. Le na chruthaíocht le uirlísí ceoil, le teicneólaíocht fuaime, agus le na éirim pearsanta tréitheach féin, thug Francach go leithbhéal eile muid in ár samhlaíocht agus meabhraíoch dár bhisiceacht timpeallachta.Tá cáil ar Jean Michel Jarre ar fud na cruinne mar gheall ar a chuid ceólchuirmeacha mhórthaibhseachta faion spéir bunaithe ar láithreáin nó ionaid stairiúla ar fud an domhain, áiteacha mar Pirimíd na h-Éigipte agus an Acropolis in Athens na Gréige. Ní ón ngaoith ná ón ngrian a fuair sé a chuid talant; is mac é le Maurice Jarre, an cumadóir clúiteach ceóil a scriobh an ceol do scanáin mhóra, in a measc Lawrence of Arabia, Dr Zhivago *agus, ag filleadh aríst ar an bfharraige, agus ar chósta na h-Éireann,* Ryan's Daughter.*

Jean Michel Jarre

Much of Ireland's oyster production is sold in France. This simply confirms the wise judgement of the French and their great reputation for celebrating the many wonders of nature—whether through their fine cuisine or priceless works of art. By his creativity with musical instruments and the technology of sound, a contemporary Frenchman has brought us to another level of awareness of our natural and physical environment. Jean Michel Jarre is now famous for his spectacular outdoor concerts, based on historic sites around the world, such as the Pyramids of Egypt and the Acropolis in Athens. His father, Maurice, wrote the music for many films, including *Lawrence of Arabia, Dr Zhivago* and, to return to coastal scenes, *Ryan's Daughter.*

Finger food

Coole Park 1896

Lady Gregory (1852–1932)

Augusta Persse a bhí ar an mbean uasal seo sular phós sí Sir William Gregory, agus bhí cónaí orthu sa teach mór a bhíodh anseo i bPáirc an Chúil in aice leis an nGort (Gort Inse Guaire). Bhí Lady Gregory ar dhuine de bhunaitheoirí an Irish Literary Theatre, *as ar tháinig an Abbey Theatre (Amharclann na Mainistreach). Anseo i bPáirc an Chúil a thugadh sí le chéile go leor de cheannródaithe an Irish Literary Revival i ndeireadh an 19ú céad. Ba é Yeats a chomhairligh di béaloideas an cheantair a bhailiú agus drámaí a scríobh ar an ábhar. Tá siúlóid bhreá sa choill anseo agus tugann go leor daoine cuairt ar an áit, tar éis dóibh béile blasta oisrí a ithe i nDroichead an Chláirín.*

Lady Gregory (1852–1932)

Augusta Persse, better known as Lady Gregory, was a co-founder of the Irish Literary Theatre, later called the Abbey. This was an important contribution to the Irish literary revival of the time. Unusually for a descendant of the landlord class, she studied old Gaelic legends, collected folklore and wrote plays based on themes of local interest. Her house at Coole Park, alas no longer standing, became a home of culture, a haven of peace and reflection for leading figures in the Irish Literary Revival of the late 19th century. Today Coole Park's woods and walkways still offer a quiet retreat, ideal if you have done too much oystering and roistering in Clarinbridge.

Lady Gregory oysters *(Oysters in Champagne)*

*I could visualise Lady Gregory enjoying this snack under the shade of her famous
Autograph Tree, the copper beech in Coole Park.*

Serves 4

16–24 cupped oysters, shells removed,
    juices strained and reserved
4 crusty bread rolls

110 g/4 oz butter, melted
90 ml/3 fl oz Champagne
90 ml/3 fl oz cream

Method

Preheat the oven to 200°C/400°F/gas mark 6. Cut the bread rolls in half. Scoop out the centres if you wish.
Brush the inside of the rolls with the melted butter and crisp them in the oven (about 4 minutes).

Pour the oyster juices into a saucepan over a low heat. Simmer until the juices are reduced by half. Add the
Champagne and cream and stir until the sauce thickens. Add the oysters to the sauce and heat them through
(2–3 minutes). Don't overcook the oysters, just warm them.

To serve

Spoon the oyster mixture on to the bread rolls and enjoy with a glass of Champagne, of course!

Tullira Castle oysters *(Hot brandy oysters)*

Serves 4

16–24 cupped oysters, shells removed,
    juices strained and reserved
freshly ground black pepper
25 g/1 oz butter
1 tablespoon shallots, finely chopped

2 tablespoons brandy
1 teaspoon lemon juice
225 ml/8 fl oz cream
salt
Garnish
warm toast

Method

Sprinkle some pepper over the oysters. Melt the butter in a saucepan and gently fry the oysters for 1–2 minutes until plump and firm. Remove the oysters from the saucepan and cover to keep warm.

Sauté the shallots in the saucepan over a moderately high heat, adding more butter if necessary. Add the brandy, oyster juices and lemon juice and stir continuously until the sauce is reduced by a third. Add the cream, salt and pepper and allow the sauce to thicken a little.

Add the oysters to the sauce and warm them through for 2–3 minutes. If you overcook the oysters, they will become tough.

To serve

Spoon the oysters on to warm toast.

Tullira Castle

Tullira Castle

Tullira Castle is on the left of the Gort–Ennis road. Built during the 15th century on the site of a much older castle, it was acquired by a branch of the Martyn family around 1600. The Martyns built the present two-storey castellated mansion in the 1870s and integrated the older tower house building with the new structure. The tower house inspired Yeats to buy his own, in Ballylee.

Caisleán Thul Oidhre

Tá Caisleán Thul Oidhre ar thaobh na láimhe clé den bhóthar ón nGort go hInis. Sa 15ú haois a tógadh é ar láthair caisleáin eile a bhí níos sine, agus a tháinig i seilbh na Máirtíneach (Martyns) thart ar 1600. Is iad na Máirtínigh seo a thóg an caisleán atá inniu ann thart ar an mbliain 1870, agus choinníodar an seanteach túir ón gcéad chaisleán mar chuid den fhoirgneamh nua. Deirtear gurb é an teach túir sin a spreag an file Yeats lena theach túir féin a cheannach i mBaile Uí Lí.

Maree oysters *(Oysters, bacon and mushrooms on a skewer)*

Serves 4

12 large oysters, shells removed,
    juices strained and reserved
6 thin streaky bacon rashers, rinds removed,
    cut in half and stretched
12 button mushrooms
1 large egg

2–3 tablespoons fine breadcrumbs
pinch of salt
pinch of cayenne pepper
Accompaniments
1 recipe Irish potato cakes (see recipe below)
melted butter

Method

Preheat the grill to high or preheat the oven to 220°C/425°F/gas mark 7. Wrap half a rasher around each oyster. Slip three oysters on to a skewer, with a mushroom between each one. Repeat with the remaining oysters and mushrooms.

Beat the egg in a bowl. Put the breadcrumbs in another bowl and mix in the salt and cayenne pepper. Dip each skewer in the beaten egg and then in the breadcrumbs. Grill until golden in colour (5–6 minutes), turning over a few times to cook evenly. Alternatively, bake the skewers in the oven for 10–12 minutes, turning often.

To serve

Serve hot with Irish potato cakes and melted butter.

Irish potato cakes

225 g/8 oz potatoes, boiled and mashed
50 g/2 oz plain flour
25 g/1 oz butter, melted

pinch of salt
sunflower oil and butter for frying

Method

Mix the mashed potatoes, flour, butter and salt together in a bowl. Turn out on to a floured board. Divide the mixture in two and shape each piece into a round. Crimp the edges and cut into triangles. Fry in a sizzling mixture of oil and butter until both sides are golden. Serve hot.

Oriental-style oysters

This is also a great starter for a Chinese meal.

Serves 4

12–16 oysters in shells, scrubbed
1 small carrot, grated
1 thin slice of fresh ginger, finely grated
2 tablespoons light soy sauce

1 tablespoon sherry
½–1 teaspoon Tabasco
1–2 teaspoons sesame oil
2 scallions (green onions), cut into fine strips
Garnish
sprigs of parsley or coriander

Method

Blanch the carrot in boiling water for 1 minute, adding the ginger for the last few seconds of blanching. Drain. Mix the soy sauce, sherry, Tabasco and sesame oil together in a bowl. Mix in the carrot, ginger and scallions.
Steam the oysters until the shells open slightly (3–4 minutes, depending on size). Using an oyster knife, twist off the top shell.

To serve

Arrange the oysters on a platter and spoon the sauce over them. Garnish with parsley or coriander and serve immediately.

Kinvara oysters *(Oysters in bacon)*

This is one of the best ever finger foods and another version of angels on horseback. It is better to par cook de-rinded bacon rashers first before using them for wrapping the oysters, to make sure they are fully cooked.

Serves 4

12 oysters, shells removed
6 streaky bacon rashers, rinds removed,
    cut in half and stretched

Garnishes

6 slices of toast, buttered and cut into triangles
sprigs of watercress or parsley

Method

Preheat the grill to high or the oven to 220°C/425°F/gas mark 7. Wrap the bacon around the oysters and slip on to skewers to secure. Grill or bake the oysters for 5–6 minutes, turning occasionally to cook evenly.

To serve

Remove the oysters from the skewers and arrange on the triangles of toast. Garnish with watercress or parsley and serve immediately.

Note: you can plump up the oysters by heating them in their own juices for a minute or two before wrapping the bacon around them.

Kinvara

Known in Irish as *'Cinn Mhara'*, the head of the sea, this village is aptly named being the furthest inward point reached by the waters of Galway Bay. In former times, Kinvara carried out a lively sea trading business with villages on the north side of the bay. This is now commemorated annually through the *Cruinniú na mBád*, or the Gathering of the Boats festival. Kinvara is also the birthplace of Francis P. Fahy (1854–1935) who wrote many well-known ballads, including the older, pre-Bing Crosby version of 'Galway Bay'.

Cinn Mhara

Chuala go leor de pháistí scoile na hÉireann faoi Chinn Mhara, nuair a léigh siad scéal cáiliúil Phádraig Uí Chonaire M'Asal Beag Dubh, a thosaíonn leis na línte: 'I gCinn Mhara a bhíos nuair a chuireas aithne ar m'asal beag dubh i dtosach.' Seans maith gur i mbád móna a tháinig Sean-Phádraig as Ros Muc go Cinn Mhara, mar go mbíodh go leor de na Báid Mhóra as Conamara ag dul go Cinn Mhara le móin ag an am, sular thóg na leoraithe áit na mbád mór. Déantar ceiliúradh ar an seanchaidreamh tráchtála idir an 'taobh thiar' agus an 'taobh thoir' gach samhradh le roinnt bhlianta anois, ag féile 'Chruinniú na mBád' i gCinn Mhara. Ar an mbaile seo freisin a rugadh Francis P. Fahy (1854–1935), an fear a chum an seanleagan de 'Galway Bay'.

Galway Bay oysters *(Oysters baked in mushrooms)*

This is wonderful finger food for a drinks party or for brunch. It also makes great pub grub and can be served with chips.

Serves 4

12 oysters, shells removed
12 large mushrooms
paprika
175 g/6 oz butter, melted

Topping

50 g/2 oz butter
2 tablespoons fine breadcrumbs
2 tablespoons grated Parmesan cheese or Irish Cheddar
squares of hot buttered toast

Method

Preheat the oven to 220°C/425°F/gas mark 7. Place a baking tray in the oven. Wipe the mushrooms clean and remove the stems. Sprinkle each mushroom cap with a little paprika. Spoon some melted butter over each mushroom and top with the oysters. Mix the topping ingredients together in a bowl until well combined. Divide the topping between the mushrooms. Place the mushrooms on the preheated baking tray and bake until golden (5–7 minutes).

To serve

Place the mushrooms on the squares of toast and serve immediately.

Cormac's oysters *(Steamed beer oysters)*

Beer steam imparts a very special flavour to oysters.

Serves 4
24 oysters in shells, scrubbed
1–2 x 500 ml cans lager beer
8–10 whole peppercorns
1 bay leaf
3–6 whole cloves

Accompaniments
1 recipe cocktail sauce (see recipe below)
1 recipe tartare sauce (see page 83)
1 recipe garlic butter (see page 83)
sea vegetable muffins (see page 120)
pure Irish butter

Method
Pour the beer into a large, wide, shallow saucepan or a roasting dish. Add the peppercorns, bay leaf and cloves. Place the oysters curved side down in the beer and bring to boiling point. Steam the oysters for 6–8 minutes until the shells open slightly. The steaming can be done on top of the cooker or in a hot oven (220°C/425°F/gas mark 7). Lift the oysters carefully from the pan.

To serve
Put the cocktail and tartare sauces and garlic butter in small dishes in the middle of a large platter and arrange the oysters around them. Serve with plenty of sea vegetable muffins and butter and glasses of cold beer.

Cocktail sauce

4–5 tablespoons mayonnaise
   (see recipe above or use shop-bought)
2–3 tablespoons tomato ketchup
1–2 tablespoons whipped cream

dash of lemon juice
dash of Worcester sauce
3–4 drops Tabasco sauce

Method
Mix all of the ingredients together. Cover and chill until ready to serve.

Note: you can adjust the amounts depending on your taste—for example, doubling the amount of mayonnaise will make a milder sauce.

Tartare sauce

4 tablespoons mayonnaise
    (see recipe above or use shop-bought)
½ teaspoon finely chopped chives
½ teaspoon chopped capers
½ small gerkin, chopped

½ teaspoon fresh chervil
½ teaspoon fresh tarragon
¼ teaspoon mustard
½–1 tablespoon wine vinegar (enough to taste)

Method
Mix all the ingredients well together, cover and refrigerate for at least half an hour before serving. Serve in a clean oyster shell.

Garlic butter

50 g/2 oz butter

1 clove garlic, crushed

Method
Blend the butter and garlic together until smooth.

Connacht Gold oysters *(Baked oysters in savoury butter)*

Serves 4
24 oysters in half shells
110 g/4 oz butter, softened

1–2 tablespoons toasted pine nuts, crushed (optional)
1 tablespoon basil, chopped
1 tablespoon lemon juice

Method
Mix all the ingredients except the oysters together in a bowl until well combined. Chill for at least 10 minutes.
Preheat the oven to 220°C/425°F/gas mark 7. Place a knob of the chilled butter mixture on top of each oyster. Place on a baking tray and bake until sizzling and juicy (4–5 minutes). Serve hot.

Connacht Gold oysters

Mike's oysters *(Oyster fritters)*

Serves 4
24 oysters, shells removed and retained,
    juices strained and reserved
2 tablespoons olive oil
2 teaspoons lemon juice
salt, freshly ground black pepper
1 recipe tempura batter (see recipe below)
oil for deep frying.

Dipping sauce 1
4–6 tablespoons soy sauce
4–6 tablespoons water
juice of 1 large lemon or lime
Dipping sauce 2
1 part soy sauce
2 parts mirin sauce
a few drops of hot chilli oil
Garnish
lemon wedges

Method
Make the tempura batter, choosing the recipe you prefer.
Mix the olive oil, lemon juice and seasoning in a bowl. Poach the oysters for a few seconds in their own juices until plump and curled at the edges. Remove the oysters from the saucepan, reserving the juices. Marinate the oysters in the oil and lemon for about half an hour. Remove and pat them dry. Dip the oysters in the batter and deep fry in hot oil (190°C/375°F) until puffed and golden (2–3 minutes). Drain on kitchen paper.
Mix the dipping sauce ingredients together and pour into small bowls.

To serve
Place the hot fritters in the clean oyster shells and serve with lemon wedges and the dipping sauces.

Tempura batter 1

1 egg
150 ml/5 fl oz iced water
110 g/4 oz plain flour

Lightly whisk the egg and iced water.
Add the flour all at once and mix well,
leaving the batter a little lumpy.

Tempura batter 2

50 g/2 oz plain flour
50 g/2 oz corn flour
pinch salt
150 ml/5 fl oz ice cold soda water (from new bottle)

Mix all the the dry ingredients together and pour in the soda water. Mix gently, leaving the mixture a little lumpy.

Galway Blazer oysters *(Curried oysters)*

Serves 4

24 oysters, shells removed and retained,
    juices reserved
2 shallots, finely chopped
1 clove garlic, crushed
25 g/1 oz butter, melted
4 tablespoons cream
pinch of cayenne pepper
pinch of saffron

1–2 teaspoons curry powder
1 teaspoon lemon juice
Garnish
lemon wedges
Accompaniments
brown scones (see page 122)
butter

Method

Poach the oysters for a few seconds in their own juices until plump and curled at the edges. Strain and reserve the juice for the sauce.

Sauté the shallots and garlic in a saucepan with the melted butter for 2–3 minutes. Add the oyster juices and cook until the liquid is reduced by half. Add the cream, cayenne pepper, saffron, curry powder and lemon juice. Whisk continuously over a medium heat until the sauce thickens.

Preheat the grill to high. Put the oysters back in their shells and cover them with the sauce. Grill until golden on top (2–3 minutes).

To serve

Serve with lemon wedges, scones and butter.

Willie Moran's oysters

Serves 4

12–18 plump oysters, in half shells with juices
50 g/2 oz butter, melted

50 g/2 oz fine breadcrumbs
50 g/2 oz Cheddar cheese, grated (optional)

Method

Preheat the grill to high. Fry the breadcrumbs in the melted butter until golden. Mix the cheese (if using) into the crumb mixture and spoon over the oysters. Grill until golden and sizzling (3–4 minutes). Serve immediately.

Avonmore oysters *(Oysters with basil and garlic butter)*

Serves 4

12–18 oysters
110 g/4 oz butter

1 clove garlic, crushed
1 teaspoon basil, finely chopped
50 g/2 oz Cheddar or Doolin cheese, grated

Method

Preheat the grill to high. Blend the butter, garlic and basil until smooth. Top each oyster with some of the butter mixture and sprinkle with a little cheese. Place on a baking tray or grill pan and grill until golden on top (2–3 minutes).

Note: you can substitute parsley for basil.

Glazed Burren oysters *(Oysters with mature Doolin cheese)*

Serves 4

16–24 oysters in half shells
6–8 tablespoons cream

freshly ground black pepper
1–2 tablespoons mature Doolin cheese (or Cheddar), grated
25 g/1 oz butter, melted

Method

Preheat the grill to high. Loosen the oysters in their shells and place them on the grill pan. Spoon over some cream and sprinkle with a little black pepper. Sprinkle with cheese and dribble a little melted butter on top. Grill until golden (2–3 minutes).

Willie Moran's oyster cottage

A thatched cottage, gently flowing tide, stately swans, a picturesque countryside including a view of an old oyster fishery. This is the setting for Willie Moran's Oyster Cottage and Seafood Bar at the Weir, Kilcolgan, off the N18. Fishing, farming and catering have been in the family for generations. The current owner, Willie Moran, has won International Oyster Opening Championships on more than one occasion. The native oyster is his pride and joy, served with reverence when in season and of course, the gigas are on the menu all year round.

Teach Willie Moran

Teach ceann tuí le hais beirtreach oisrí, agus an eala ar an lán mara lena thaobh. Sin é an suíomh atá ar thabhairne oisrí Willie Moran i gCill Cholgáin, isteach de bhóthar an N18, ó dheas as Gaillimh. Tá bia mara agus bia feirme á réiteach sa teach seo le fada an lá, agus tá Craobhchomórtais Idirnáisiúnta Oscailt Oisrí buaite arís agus arís eile ag fear an tí, Willie Moran. Is é an t-oisre áitiúil is ansa leis féin a thabhairt dá chuid custaiméirí, ach bíonn an cineál eile oisrí (giga) ar an mbiachlár anseo i gcaitheamh na bliana go léir.

Oysters with beer drop scones

Cill Chiaráin oysters *(Grilled oysters)*

Serves 4

12–24 Cill Chiaráin oysters in half shells
6–8 tablespoons cream
1–2 tablespoons Cheddar or farmhouse
    cheese, grated

50g/2 oz butter, melted
50g/2 oz fine bread crumbs
cayenne pepper

Method

Preheat the grill to high. Remove the oysters from their shells and drain. Put the shells on the grill pan and spoon a little cream into each one. Return the oysters to their shells. Cover each one with some cheese, butter and breadcrumbs. Sprinkle a little cayenne pepper on top and grill until golden (2–3 minutes).

Note: crushed tinfoil on the grill pan will keep the oysters steady while cooking..

Kilkieran

Kilkieran is on the north coast of Galway Bay in the heartland of the Connemara Gaeltacht where Irish is the spoken language. Oysters from this area have special qualities and we have a saint's word for that. Local folklore has it that when in the 6th century St Kieran was on the Aran Islands he longed for oysters. There were none on Aran, so he set sail for the mainland. He survived a stormy crossing and was driven ashore at Kilkieran, where he built a church in thanksgiving. St Kieran's feast day is still commemorated on 9 September—just when the oyster season starts to roll.

Cill Chiaráin

Siar ó Ros Muc go Carna atá Cill Chiaráin, baile atá ainmnithe i ndiaidh Naomh Ciarán, a tháinig anseo sa séú haois, ar a bhealach go hÁrainn. Ní scéal nua ar bith é go bhfuil oisrí den scoth ar an mbeirtreach anseo, agus tá scéal ón mbéaloideas go raibh Naomh Ciarán ceanúil ar na hoisrí céanna. Le linn dó a bheith in Árainn bhuail dúil sna hoisrí é, agus ó tharla nach raibh aon oisre le fáil sna hoileáin, d'ardaigh sé a sheolta in aghaidh stoirme agus gála, gur bhain sé Cill Chiaráin amach agus gur bhain sé a dhúil as na hoisrí. Thóg sé an chill ansin, mar bhuíochas do Dhia a thug slán trasna an chuain é. Comórtar Lá Fhéile Ciaráin ar an 9ú lá de Mheán Fómhair, tráth a mbíonn séasúr na n-oisrí agus Féile na n-Oisrí ina reacht seoil.

Pan-fried oysters on toasted bagels

A nice breakfast or brunch.

Serves 4

12–16 oysters, drained and shells removed
25 g/1 oz butter

50 g/2 oz creamy goats' cheese
4 bagels, halved, toasted and buttered

Method

Fry the oysters in foaming butter for about 1 minute. Spread the cheese on the hot buttered bagels and place the oysters on top.

Mushroom and oyster fritters

Serves 4

24 oysters, drained, shells removed and retained
300 ml/10 fl oz pancake batter (see page 62)
24 button mushrooms
plain flour for dusting

salt, freshly ground black pepper
sunflower/vegetable oil for deep frying
Garnish
tartare sauce (see page 83)

Method

Wash and dry the oyster shells and set aside. Make the pancake batter and set it aside in the fridge. Wipe the mushrooms and trim off the very end of the stalks. Season the flour with salt and pepper. Toss the oysters in the flour. Dip the mushrooms and oysters in the batter and then plunge them into very hot oil—180–190°C/350–375°F—and fry until crisp and golden.

To serve

Place the fried oysters in their shells, top each with a mushroom and serve with tartare sauce.

Paddy Burke's oysters *(Fried oysters with spicy sausage toast)*

Serves 4

12–18 oysters, shells removed and retained
3–4 Connemara lamb sausages, casings removed
4–8 slices buttered toast
3–4 tablespoons fine breadcrumbs

sunflower oil for frying
Garnish
Tabasco or lemon wedges or a sauce of your choice
(see recipes above)

Method

Preheat the grill to high. Preheat the oven to 180°C/350°F/gas mark 4. Spread the sausage meat on the toast, ensuring that it is spread out to the edges. Grill until the sausage meat is cooked and sizzling (2–3 minutes). Keep warm in the oven. Toss the oysters in breadcrumbs and fry in hot oil until firm, plump and golden.

To serve

Place a few oysters on each sausage toast and serve while hot with Tabasco, lemon wedges or sauce. The sauce can be served in a clean, dry oyster shell.

Tigh Phaddy Burke

Ceannródaí a bhí in Paddy Burke, nach maireann, duine de na chéad tabhairneoirí a chuir oisrí ina leathshliogáin ar fáil dá chuid custaiméirí ina theach tabhairne cáiliúil anseo i nDroichead an Chláirín. Ba é freisin a d'eagraigh agus a reachtáil an chéad fhéile oisrí ar an mbaile anseo i 1954. Cé gur úinéirí eile atá ar an tabhairne anois, tá an t-ainm 'Paddy Burke's' ar an teach fós, agus is é croílár Fhéile na nOisrí i gcónaí é. Tagann daoine ann ó chían agus ó chongar, ó cheann ceann na bliana.

Paddy Burke's

The late Paddy Burke was a truly pioneering spirit. He was one of the first publicans to serve oysters in their half-shells at the counter bar of his pub in Clarinbridge. He was also host, sponsor and organiser of the village's first Oyster Festival in 1954. The pub has since passed to other hands but Paddy Burke's is still the hub of Galway oystering festivities and a popular place for food and drink all year round.

Carna oysters grilled

Serves 4

24 Carna oysters, drained and shells removed
12 small streaky bacon rashers
50 g/2 oz butter, melted
juice of a large lemon
salt, freshly ground black pepper
pinch of cayenne pepper

24 small button mushrooms
1 tablespoon cornflour
Garnish
lemon wedges
Accompaniment
hot buttered toast

Method

Preheat the grill or barbecue to high. De-rind, stretch and par-cook the bacon rashers on the grill for 2–3 minutes. (The par-cooking ensures that the bacon is cooked through.) Remove from the heat and cut in two. Mix the butter with the lemon juice and seasoning. Dip the oysters and mushrooms in the butter mixture and then in the cornflour. Skewer the oysters, mushrooms and rolled-up bacon, leaving room between each piece for grilling. Grill or barbecue until golden.

To serve

Serve the skewers on hot buttered toast.

Deep-fried oyster and sausage bouchées

Galway Bay oysters with prawns

Serves 4

12–18 Galway Bay oysters in half shells, with juices
Sauce
110 g/4 oz prawns
50 g/2 oz butter, melted
50 g/2 oz button mushrooms, finely chopped
2 tablespoons plain flour or cornflour
1 tablespoon onion, finely chopped
1 tablespoon celery, finely chopped

1 tablespoon dry sherry or white wine
dash of Worcestershire sauce
dash of Tabasco
1 clove of garlic, finely chopped
Topping
50 g/2 oz fine breadcrumbs
75 g/3 oz butter, melted
50 g/2 oz Cheddar cheese, grated (optional)

Method
Preheat the grill to high. Place the oysters on some crumpled tinfoil on a large baking tray and flash under the grill for about 2 minutes or until the edges curl. Remove from the grill and strain the juices into a bowl. Put all the sauce ingredients and the oyster juices into a food processor and blend until smooth. Pour the mixture into a saucepan and stir over a low heat until the sauce has a thick, creamy consistency.
Spoon the sauce over the oysters and cover with a mixture of breadcrumbs, melted butter and cheese (if using). Grill until the tops are golden and the oysters are heated through, about 3–4 minutes.

Renvyle oysters *(Oysters in hot cream)*

Serves 4

16–24 oysters in half shells
6–8 tablespoons cream
freshly ground black pepper

1–2 tablespoons Cheddar or farmhouse cheese, grated
25 g/1 oz butter, melted

Method
Preheat the grill to high. Loosen the oysters in their shells and carefully place them on the grill pan. Spoon a little cream over each one and sprinkle with pepper. Sprinkle some cheese on top and dribble the melted butter over each oyster. Grill until golden (2–3 minutes).

Oysters with beer drop scones

Serves 4

12 oysters, juices strained and reserved,
    oysters chopped

Beer batter

225 g/8 oz plain flour
1 teaspoon baking powder
¼ teaspoon salt
pinch of cayenne pepper
250 ml/8 fl oz milk
125 ml/4 fl oz cream

1 large egg
1 egg yolk
2 tablespoons ale
butter and sunflower oil for frying

Garnishes

sour cream
small bunch of chives, chopped

Method

Sieve the flour, baking powder, salt and cayenne pepper into a large bowl. Make a well in the centre and add the milk, cream, egg, egg yolk and ale. Beat vigorously to make a smooth batter. Leave to rest for about 30 minutes. Add the chopped oysters, with their juices, to the beer batter. Mix gently. Melt a small knob of butter and a small drop of oil in a frying pan and, when hot, fry the oyster batter in spoonfuls. Cook on both sides until golden.

To serve

Serve topped with sour cream and chives.

Deep-fried oyster and sausage *bouchées*

This is dream finger food.

Serves 4

18–24 oysters, drained and shells removed
1–2 tablespoons plain flour
salt, freshly ground black pepper
225 g/8 oz sausages, casings removed

2 medium eggs, beaten
110 g/4 oz fine breadcrumbs
sunflower oil for deep frying

Method

Preheat the oil to 180–190ºC/350–375°F. Chill the oysters to firm them. Season the flour with salt and pepper and toss the oysters in the flour. Make small flat circles of the sausage meat. Encase each oyster in sausage meat and seal well. Dip the encased oysters in the beaten egg and then in the breadcrumbs. Deep fry in the hot oil for 3–4 minutes or until the outer casing is crisp.

Note: the oysters can be poached in their own juices for 1–2 minutes before being encased—this will plump them up.

Oyster croque monsieur

This is my Irish version of the famous French snack, so popular at lunchtime.

Serves 4

8 oysters, shells removed and juices reserved
8 slices of Cheddar cheese
8 slices of buttered bread

4 slices of cooked ham
50 g/2 oz unsalted butter for frying

Method

Poach the oysters for 1–2 minutes in their own juices. Drain and chop. Place a slice of cheese on a slice of buttered bread. Place a slice of ham over the cheese and spread the chopped oysters over the ham. Cover with a second slice of cheese and lastly a slice of buttered bread. Heat the butter in a pan until it froths, then skim the froth off to make clarified butter. Fry the croques in the clarified butter until golden brown on each side.

To serve

Cut into triangles and serve hot.

Oysters with sour cream topping

Serves 4

12–24 oysters in half shells
110 g/4 oz butter, melted
1 tablespoon sunflower oil
1 clove of garlic, crushed

110 g/4 oz fine breadcrumbs
3 tablespoons sour cream
1 tablespoon Cheddar cheese, grated

Method

Preheat the grill to high. Place the oysters on some crumpled tinfoil on a large baking tray and flash under the hot grill for about 2 minutes or until the edges curl. Remove from the grill and drain off a little of the juices.

Mix together the butter, oil, garlic and breadcrumbs. Allow the mixture to cool and then fold in the sour cream and the cheese. Top the oysters with the mixture and grill until golden (3–4 minutes).

St Cleran's oysters *(Oysters with bacon and vodka)*

Serves 4

12–24 oysters in half shells
2 bacon rashers, rinds removed
1–2 tablespoons vodka
1–2 drops Tabasco

1–2 tablespoons tomato purée
dash of Worcestershire sauce
50 g/2 oz fine breadcrumbs
50 g/2 oz Cheddar cheese, grated

Method

Preheat the grill to high. Fry or grill the bacon until golden brown. Drain on kitchen paper and cut into small pieces. Put the bacon into a small bowl and add the vodka, Tabasco, tomato purée and Worcestershire sauce. Mix well.

Place the oysters on the grill pan and spoon the mixture over them. Sprinkle each one with breadcrumbs and cheese. Grill until golden on top (2–3 minutes).

John Huston at a Galway Oyster Festival

St Cleran's

Tagann daoine cáiliúla ó thionscal na scannán chuig féilte oisrí na Gaillimhe ó bhliain go bliain. Cheannaigh an stiúrthóir scannán John Huston an teach mór St Cleran's i ndeisceart na Gaillimhe i 1954, teach a tógadh ar dtús do mhuintir de Búrca i dtús an 19ú céad. Cailleadh Robert Burke in 1861, le linn dó a bheith i gceannas ar bhuíonn fear ag dul trasna ha hAstráille.

Déanann na Hustons urraíocht ar The Huston School of Digital Film and Media *in Ollscoil na hÉireann, Gaillimh.*

St Cleran's

Film celebrities were frequent visitors to Galway Oyster Festivals. John Huston, film director, bought one of the Big Houses in south Galway in 1954. This is St Cleran's, near Craughwell, which was built for the Burkes in the early 1800s. Robert Burke died leading an expedition across Australia in 1861. The Hustons are no longer at St Cleran's but their links to Galway are maintained through their sponsorship of the Huston School of Digital Film and Media at the University.

Main courses

Kevin's oyster pie

Roscam oysters *(Oysters with steak)*

What a dream marriage of land and sea this dish is. It would be very welcome after a day at the Galway Races.

Serves 4
6–8 oysters
4 x 175 g/6 oz fillet steaks
olive oil for frying

Accompaniments
baked potatoes
sour cream

Method

Slit the steaks down the middle and enclose the oysters in the centre. Fold the steaks over and secure with cocktail sticks. Fry over a high heat until the steak is cooked to your preference (about 4 minutes per side for medium-rare).

To serve

Remove the cocktail sticks and serve the steak and oysters with the baked potatoes and sour cream. Wash it down with your favourite stout.

Ros Cam

Trasna ó Aird Fhraoigh, i gcúinne thoir-thuaidh Chuan na Gaillimhe, tá Ros Cam. Tá láthair mainistreach ón séú haois anseo agus é caomhnaithe ón bhforbairt mhór atáthar a dhéanamh ar chathair na Gaillimhe. Tá iarsmaí eaglaise ó na meánaoiseanna ar an láthair, mar aon le túr cruinn atá míle bliain d'aois. Tá an túr fágtha gan díon, agus ceaptar go mb'fhéidir gur túr é nár críochnaíodh riamh. Bhí iasc agus sligiasc le fáil go flúirseach sa bhfarraige ag na manaigh anseo, agus ní raibh orthu dul i bhfad ag iarraidh béile breá oisrí.

Roscam

Across from Ardfry in the north eastern corner of Galway Bay is Roscam. Here, a monastic site dating back to the 6th century is preserved from modern suburban development extending from Galway city. On the site are the ruins of a medieval church and a roofless round tower built a thousand years ago but, some say, never completed. The monks of old lived as self-sufficient communities and doubtless, seafood, including oysters, was part of their diet.

Tom Sally's oyster stew

Serves 4

36 oysters, shells removed, juices
    strained and reserved
50 g/2 oz butter
4 bacon rashers, rinds removed, coarsely chopped
1 large onion, finely chopped
1 large potato, peeled and cut into small cubes
1 tablespoon carrageen moss, cleaned and
    finely chopped, tied in muslin

425 ml/15 fl oz milk or fish stock
1 tablespoon parsley, finely chopped
425 ml/15 fl oz cream
salt, freshly ground black pepper
Garnish
fingers of hot buttered toast or croûtons

Method

Melt the butter in a large saucepan, add the bacon and onion and sauté until the onion is translucent. Add the potatoes and carrageen moss and mix. Pour in the oyster juices and milk and simmer gently until the potatoes are soft. Stir in the parsley and cream. Add the oysters and simmer gently for 2–3 minutes until the oysters are plump and the cream is warmed. Remove the carrageen parcel and season with salt and pepper.

To serve

Ladle the stew into warm bowls and serve with toast or croûtons.

Note: you can add more milk or cream if the stew is too thick.

Lord Wallscourt stew

Serves 4

12–18 oysters, shells removed, juices
    strained and reserved
50 g/2 oz butter
3–4 bacon rashers, rinds removed,
    coarsely chopped
1 leek (white part only), finely chopped
1 stalk celery, finely chopped
1 large potato, peeled and chopped into small cubes

5–6 mushrooms, sliced thinly
425 ml/15 fl oz milk
425 ml/15 fl oz cream
2 tablespoons parsley, finely chopped
salt, freshly ground black pepper
Garnish
crunchy croûtons or fingers of hot buttered toast

Method

Melt the butter in a large saucepan and fry the bacon for 2–3 minutes over medium heat. Add the vegetables and sauté for a further 2–3 minutes.
Add the oyster juices and milk and simmer gently until the potato cubes are soft. Add the cream, parsley and oysters and gently cook until warmed through (about 2 minutes). Season to taste.

To serve

Ladle the stew into warm bowls. Sprinkle with croûtons or toast.

Lord Wallscourt

Ba mhinic achrann faoi chúrsaí cíosa idir na tiarnaí talún agus na tionóntaí in Éirinn, ach tharla achrann de chineál eile i ndeireadh an 19ú céad, nuair a shocraigh rialtas na linne, den chéad uair, beirtreacha oisrí thart leis an gcósta a thabhairt le saothrú go príobháideach. Ba iad na húinéirí móra talún a fuair na ceadúnais. Ach níor ghéill na tionóntaí a gcearta chun na n-oisrí go héasca, agus b'éigean do na tiarnaí talún báillí a fhostú chun na tionóntaí a choinneáil ó na hoisrí. Bhain tionóntaí áirithe cáil mhór amach mar phóitseálaithe. Bronnadh na chéad cheadúnais oisrí i gCuan na Gaillimhe ar Lord Wallscourt agus ar bheirt de na St Georges, William agus James.

Lord Wallscourt

Relationships between landlords and tenant farmers were never very peaceful in Ireland. They took a turn for the worse in the late 19th century as the government sought to promote oyster cultivation—as distinct from oyster gathering—by privatising oyster beds. Licences were granted mostly to the big landowners, those being deemed capable of stocking and managing the beds. But they had to employ bailiffs to protect what locals still regarded as their own, while resourceful poachers became local heroes. Two of the earliest licences in Galway Bay were given to Lord Wallscourt and to the St Georges, William and James.

Connemara oyster casserole *(Oyster and potato casserole)*

Serves 4

12–16 oysters, shells removed,
    juices strained and reserved
4–5 large potatoes (about 1 kg/2 lb), peeled
1–5 bacon rashers, rinds removed
600 ml/16 fl oz oyster juices and cream, combined
1 large onion, finely chopped
2 tablespoons parsley, chopped
25 g/1 oz butter, cut into small cubes

celery salt or salt
freshly ground black pepper
1 clove of garlic, finely chopped
110 g/4 oz fine breadcrumbs
225 g/8 oz Cheddar cheese, grated

Garnish
sprigs of parsley

Accompaniment
green salad

Method

Preheat the oven to 200°C/400°F/gas mark 6. Grease a medium-sized casserole dish. Bring the potatoes to boiling point in a saucepan, cover and simmer until cooked through, about 15 minutes. Drain, allow to cool slightly and slice. Set aside.

Fry or grill the bacon until golden brown. Drain on kitchen paper and cut into small pieces. Heat the oysters in a saucepan in their own juices until they are plump and the edges curl. Remove from the saucepan and set aside. Allow the juices to cool and then combine with the cream.

Slice the potatoes and put half of them in a layer on the bottom of the casserole dish. Add half the bacon, onions, parsley and cubes of butter. Season with salt, pepper and a little of the garlic. Add the oysters in a layer. Add the remainder of the bacon, onions, parsley and butter. Season again and finish with the rest of the potatoes.

Pour the oyster juices and cream to come three-quarters of the way up the dish. Sprinkle the top of the casserole with the breadcrumbs and cheese. Bake for about 30 minutes or until the top is golden and the dish is heated through.

To serve

Sprinkle some parsley over the top of the casserole and serve hot with the green salad.

Connemara oyster casserole

Kevin's oyster pie *(Oyster and Guinness beef pie)*

*Oysters have an affinity with many Irish ingredients, of which Irish beef is one.
Marry those two ingredients with our famous Guinness and you have a meal fit for
a king or queen.*

Serves 4

12 oysters, shells removed, juices strained
    and reserved
2 tablespoons plain flour
salt, freshly ground black pepper
700 g/1½ lb rib beef, cubed
2 tablespoons sunflower oil

1–2 onions, finely chopped
225 g/8 oz mushrooms, chopped
425 ml/15 fl oz Guinness
1 tablespoon Worcestershire sauce
200 g/7 oz ready-made puff pastry
Accompaniment
green salad or baked potatoes

Method

Season the flour with salt and pepper. Toss the beef in the flour. Heat the oil in a large, heavy frying pan. Once the oil is hot, add the beef to the pan a little at a time and seal. (Be careful not to overcrowd the pan as this will only create a stewing process.) Remove the beef from the pan.

Fry the onions and mushrooms until soft and then return the meat to the pan. Add the Guinness, Worcestershire sauce and oyster juices and season with salt and pepper. Mix well, cover and simmer until the meat is tender (about 1½ hours). Remove from the heat and allow to cool completely. Add the oysters.

Preheat the oven to 200°C/400°F/gas mark 6. Grease a deep pie dish. Pour the mixture into the pie dish. Cover with the pastry, leaving a slight overhang around the edge of the dish. Crimp the edges firmly and cut an air vent in the centre of the pastry.

Bake in the centre of the oven for 15 minutes. Reduce the heat to 180°C/350°F/gas mark 4 and bake for a further 30 minutes until the meat is heated through.

To serve

Serve hot with a green salad or baked potatoes.

Note: you could also make four individual pies rather than one large one.

Colcannon cake with oyster and sausage *bouchées*

Serves 4

24 oysters, shells removed and retained
225 g/8 oz potatoes
15 g/½ oz butter
25–50 g/1–2 oz cabbage, finely shredded, cooked
salt, freshly ground black pepper
4 tablespoons butter, melted

1–2 tablespoons plain flour
8–12 Connemara lamb sausages or good-quality
    butcher's sausages
1 large egg, beaten
110 g/4 oz fine breadcrumbs
sunflower oil for deep frying

Method

Boil, peel and mash the potatoes. Sauté the cabbage in a saucepan with melted butter for 3–4 minutes, then mix it with the mashed potatoes. Season to taste. Divide the cabbage and potato mixture into four pieces and flatten out to make rough rounds. Fry in hot foaming butter until golden on both sides and keep warm.

Season the flour with salt and pepper. Chill the oysters to firm them and then toss them in the seasoned flour. Make small flat circles of the sausage meat. Encase each oyster in sausage meat and seal well. Dip the encased oysters in the beaten egg and then in the breadcrumbs. Deep fry in the hot oil for 3–4 minutes or until the outer casing is crisp.

To serve

Place the potato and cabbage cakes on plates and top with the sausage *bouchées*. Serve at once.

Native Irish oysters

Ros Muc

Síneann Gaeltacht Chonamara siar le cósta ó chathair na Gaillimhe. Is cósta bearnach, mantach é, lán de ghlaschuanta foscúla, cosúil le leithinis Ros Muc anseo, agus é ag gobadh amach i gCuan Chill Chiaráin. Tá beirtreacha osrí á saothrú sa gceantar seo le blianta fada. Leathchéad bliain ó shin, chabhraigh Gael Linn le hiascairí an cheantair seo forbairt a dhéanamh ar na beirtreacha, go dtí gur bunaíodh na comharchumainn iascaireachta atá ann faoi láthair. Cáil na litríochta is mó atá ar Ros Muc, a bhuíochas sin go háirithe do Phádraig Ó Conaire (1882–1928) a tógadh san ait agus do Phádraig Mac Piarais (1879–1916), a bhfuil an teach ansin fós ina ndearna sé go leor dá chuid scríbhneoireachta agus dá chuid smaointeoireachta polaitiúil.

Rosmuc

Westward from the coastal suburbs of Galway city is south-west Connemara, a territory of severely fractured shorelines, deep inlets and smithereens of little islands. On the peninsula of Rosmuc, bordering Kilkieran Bay, oyster beds have been cultivated for over 150 years. Those beds were owned by the gentry who had to maintain a constant watch over the activities of poachers, before oyster farming passed into co-operative ownership. Two Irish literary figures are associated with Rosmuc. Pádraic Ó Conaire (1882–1928) the short story writer grew up there while Pádraic Pearse(1879–1916) bought a cottage in Rosmuc from where he wrote some of his plays and stories.

Rosmuc oyster casserole *(Oyster and potato casserole)*

This makes a very tasty lunch.

Serves 4

24 oysters, shells removed and juices reserved
4–5 large potatoes
6–8 bacon rashers
1 large onion, finely chopped
2 tablespoons parsley, chopped
1–2 cloves garlic, finely chopped

freshly ground black pepper
celery salt
50 g/2 oz butter, cut into small cubes
500 ml/16 fl oz oyster juice and cream combined
110 g/4 oz fine breadcrumbs
225 g/8 oz Cheddar cheese

Method

Preheat the oven to 200°C/400°F/gas mark 6. Poach the oysters in their juices until the edges curl and they plump. Reserve the oyster juice. Boil, peel and slice the potatoes. Grill the rashers until crisp and crumble into small pieces.

Layer a greased pie dish with the potato slices, rashers, onion, parsley, garlic, seasoning and cubes of butter. Then add a layer of oysters and repeat to finish with a layer of potatoes. Pour in the oyster juice/cream mixture to come three-quarters of the way up the dish. Sprinkle with a mixture of crumbs and cheese. Season to taste and bake for about 30 minutes or until the top is golden and the dish is heated through.

To serve

Serve at once with the salad

St George's oysters *(Oysters with ribbon pasta, cheese and ham)*

Serves 4
16–20 oysters, chopped or halved
450 g/1 lb fettuccine
140 g/5 oz cooked ham
50 g/2 oz butter
425 ml/15 fl oz single cream

150 g/5 oz Parmesan cheese
freshly ground black pepper
Garnish
chopped parsley
Accompaniment
green salad

Method
Cook the pasta in boiling salted water until *al dente* (3–5 minutes). Strain well. Cut the ham into long strips. Melt the butter in a saucepan and add the ham. Heat well. Add the oysters, cream, cheese and pepper. Mix and heat carefully until you have an even sauce.

To serve
Turn the pasta into a large, heated bowl and pour the oyster sauce over it. Serve immediately with a large bowl of salad.

Beirtreacha oisrí St George

Bhí na St Georges i gCill Cholgáin ar na chéad daoine a fuair ceadúnas feirmeoireachta oisrí in 1872, rud a tharraing go leor clampair san áit as sin go ceann breis agus céad bliain. Bhí muintir na háite míshásta go raibh a gcearta saor-iascaireachta á gceilt orthu, agus bhí póitseáil, póilínteacht agus cásanna cúirte an-choitianta. Sa deireadh thiar thall, sna 1980daí, cheannaigh an Stát na beirtreacha oisrí don phobal ó mhuintir St George, agus tá comharchumann iascairí áitiúil i bhfeighil na n-oisrí anois.

The St George oyster beds

Among the earliest licences for oyster farming was one granted to the St George family from Kilcolgan in 1872. It was a decision that drew controversy for over 100 years as locals considered it a denial of their rights to public fishing. Poaching, policing and court cases marked life in the locality. Eventually, in the 1980s the St George oyster beds were bought by the State for the public and are now managed by a local fishery co-operative.

Dublin oyster recipes

Oysters and stout—the traditional favourite

Baked rock oysters with bacon and cabbage, Guinness sabayon

This recipe was kindly given to me by Derry Clarke, chef-patron of L'Écrivain, a much-praised Michelin-starred restaurant in Dublin. It is one of his specials.

Serves 4
24 rock oysters, shells removed and retained
4 green leaves of York cabbage
salt
4 slices cured bacon, finely sliced
1 tablespoon olive oil

Guinness sabayon
2 egg yolks
150 ml/5 fl oz Guinness
dash of lemon juice
salt and freshly ground pepper
150 ml/5 fl oz clarified butter
To serve
rock salt

Method
Don't wash the oysters. Shred the cabbage finely. Place the cabbage in boiling salted water for 1 minute, strain it and run it under cold water. Fry the bacon in the olive oil until it's crisp. Place a little cabbage in the shell, place the oyster on the cabbage and top with the bacon. Set aside.

To make the sabayon, whisk the egg yolks in a metal bowl over a saucepan of simmering water. Add the Guinness very gradually, whisking all the time. Add the lemon juice and seasoning. Whisk until the mixture holds the mark of the whisk. Remove from the heat and add the clarified butter gradually in a fine stream, whisking all the time.

Preheat the oven to 180°C/350°F/gas mark 4 and the grill to high. Put the oysters on a baking tray in the oven for 3–4 minutes to warm through. Cover the oysters with the Guinness sabayon and brown them under the grill.

To serve
Serve the oysters on a bed of rock salt.

Rock oysters King Sitric

Aidan MacManus, chef-patron of the King Sitric Fish Restaurant in Howth, Co. Dublin, has a well-deserved reputation for seafood. Very generously, he gave me these, his two favourite oyster recipes.

Serves 4

24 rock oysters, shells removed and retained
50 g/2 oz dulse seaweed, shredded

50 g/2 oz smoked salmon, cut into strips
6 – 8 tablespoons Hollandaise sauce (see recipe page 61)

Method

Preheat the grill to high or the oven to 200°C/400°F/gas mark 6. Place a small amount of shredded dulse seaweed in the bottom of each shell. Place the oyster on top of the seaweed and arrange a few strips of smoked salmon on top. Grill for 1 minute or bake for 2 minutes. Now cover each oyster with a spoonful of hollandaise sauce and grill until the sauce turns golden brown. Serve immediately.

Oysters Bloody Mary

Serves 4

24 native or rock oysters in half shells
     (the smaller the oysters, the better)
6 tomatoes, blanched, skinned, deseeded
1 generous tablespoon vodka
dash of Tabasco

2 dashes of Worcestershire sauce
juice of half a lemon
1 red chilli, deseeded and diced
½ cucumber, skinned, deseeded and diced

Method

First make the Bloody Mary. Finely dice two of the tomatoes and leave to one side. Put the remaining four tomatoes in a liquidiser with the vodka, Tabasco, Worcestershire sauce, lemon juice and chilli. Liquidise. Add the two diced tomatoes and the diced cucumber to the juice and refrigerate.
Loosen the oysters and turn them in their shells. Cover with about 1 tablespoon of the liquidised mixture and chill for about 30 minutes. Serve immediately.

Breads and scones

White kombu crisps bread

225 g/8 oz white self-raising flour
2 tablespoons kombu crisps or a mixture of
    sea vegetables, chopped

1 medium egg, beaten
2 tablespoons sunflower oil
150 ml/5 fl oz milk (approx.)

Method
Preheat the oven to 190°C/375°F/gas mark 5. If using a fan oven, reduce the temperature by 10–15 degrees. Grease a 23 x 11 cm/9 x 4½ in loaf tin.
Mix the flour and sea vegetables together in a bowl. In a separate bowl mix the beaten egg and sunflower oil with the milk.
Make a well in the centre of the flour, pour in the milk mixture and mix from the centre out with a wooden spoon until all the ingredients are combined.
Pour the mixture into the loaf tin and bake in the centre of the oven for about 30 minutes. Pierce the centre with a skewer. If it comes out clean, the bread is cooked.
Cool on a wire rack.

Note: if you need a larger loaf, double the quantities and the size of the tin and bake for 45 minutes.

Quick Guinness bread

450 g/1 lb ready-made Irish brown bread mix

25 g/1 oz oat bran

25 g/1 oz wheat germ

25 g/1 oz sunflower seeds, crushed or whole

50 g/2 oz figs, chopped (optional)

2 tablespoons Irish honey

2 tablespoons blackstrap molasses

3 tablespoons sunflower oil

300 ml/10 fl oz Guinness

Method

Preheat the oven to 190ºC/375ºF/gas mark 5. If using a fan oven, reduce the temperature by 10–15 degrees.Grease a 23 x 11 cm/9 x 4½ in loaf tin.

Place the bread mix in a large bowl. Add the bran, wheat germ, sunflower seeds and figs and mix.

In a separate bowl or jug mix the honey, molasses, sunflower oil and Guinness together.

Make a well in the centre of the flour, pour in most of the liquid and mix from the centre out with a wooden spoon until all the ingredients are combined and you get a nice soft mixture—not too runny but not at all firm.

Add the remaining liquid slowly, making sure that it can be absorbed.

Pour the mixture into the tin and bake in the centre of the oven for 40–50 minutes. Cool on a wire rack.

Note: you can also divide the mixture between two smaller loaf tins and bake for 30–35 minutes.

Quick dulse brown bread

Dulse (dilisc/creathnach) *is a sea vegetable.*

450 g/1 lb ready-made Irish brown bread mix
25 g/1 oz wheat germ
25 g/1 oz oat bran
2 tablespoons dulse, finely chopped or ground

1 tablespoon pinhead oatmeal
425 ml/15 fl oz fresh or sour milk
3 tablespoons sunflower oil

Method
Preheat the oven to 200°C/400°F/gas mark 6. Grease a 23 x 11 cm/9 x 4½ in loaf tin. Mix all the dry ingredients together in a bowl. Mix the milk and oil together in a jug. Make a well in the centre of the flour mixture, pour in the liquid and mix from the centre out with a wooden spoon until all the ingredients are combined and the consistency is quite wet. Pour the mixture into the loaf tin and bake in the centre of the oven for 40–50 minutes until the loaf sounds hollow when tapped. Cool on a wire rack.

Quick cheese bread

450 g/1 lb self-raising flour
110 g/4 oz Irish cheese, grated
2 medium eggs, beaten

4 tablespoons sunflower oil
1 teaspoon Irish mustard (optional)
300 ml/10 fl oz milk (approx.)

Method
Preheat the oven to 200°C/400°F/gas mark 6. Grease a 23 x 11 cm/9 x 4½ inch loaf tin. Mix the flour and cheese together in a bowl. Mix the beaten eggs, oil and mustard together and pour the mixture into the centre of the flour with enough milk to make a very soft dough (too soft to handle). Pour the mixture into the loaf tin and bake in the centre of the oven for about 50 minutes. Pierce the centre with a skewer and, if it comes out clean, the bread is done. Cool on a wire rack.

Sea vegetable muffins

225 g/8 oz white self-raising flour
2 tablespoons sea vegetables,
       finely chopped (kombu/dulse)

1 medium egg, beaten
3 tablespoons sunflower oil
150 ml/5 fl oz milk

Method
Preheat the oven to 190ºC/375ºF/gas mark 5. Grease six muffin tins. Mix the flour and sea vegetables together in a bowl. Mix the beaten egg with the oil and a few tablespoons of the milk. Make a well in the centre of the flour, pour in the egg mixture and mix from the centre out with a wooden spoon. Add enough of the remaining milk to make a very soft dough. Spoon the mixture into greased muffin tins and bake in the centre of the oven for 15–20 minutes. Remove from the tin and cool on a wire rack.

Note: cheese muffins can be made by replacing the sea vegetables with 2 oz of grated Irish Cheddar.

Traditional brown soda bread

110 g/4 oz plain flour
½ teaspoon salt
½ teaspoon bread soda

350 g/12 oz wholemeal flour
300 ml/10 fl oz (approx.) sour milk or buttermilk

Method
Preheat the oven to 200°C/400°F/gas mark 6. Grease a flat baking tray. Sieve the flour, salt and bread soda in a bowl, then mix in the flour thoroughly. Make a well in the centre of the flour, pour in the milk and mix from the centre out to make a soft dough. Turn out on to a floured board and knead until smooth underneath. Turn the smooth side up and flatten to a round of 5 cm/2 in thick. Place the dough on the baking tray and cut a cross on the top. Bake for 40 minutes or until the bread gives a hollow sound when the base is tapped. Cool on a wire rack.

Note: one tablespoon of bran, wheat germ or oatmeal may be added to the dry ingredients for extra roughage.

Quick brown bread

350 g/12 oz self-raising brown flour
110 g/4 oz self-raising white flour
25 g/1 oz bran
25 g/1 oz pinhead oatmeal

25 g/1 oz wheat germ
25 g/1 oz caster sugar
425 ml/15 fl oz sour or fresh milk
3 tablespoons sunflower oil

Method
Preheat the oven to 200°C/400°F/gas mark 6. Grease a 23 x 11 cm/9 x 4½ in loaf tin.
Mix all the dry ingredients together in a bowl. Mix the milk and oil together in a jug.
Make a well in the centre of the flour mixture, pour in the liquid and mix from the centre out with a wooden spoon until you have a soft dough.
Pour the mixture into the tin and bake in the centre of the oven for about 40 minutes.
Cool on a wire rack.

Note: if you don't have self-raising flour, mix half a teaspoon of bread soda (without any lumps) into the flour and use sour milk only.

Brown scones

110g/4oz plain white flour
½ teaspoon salt
½ teaspoon breadsoda
350 g/12 oz wholemeal flour

1 teaspoon sugar (optional)
300 ml/½ pint (approx) sour milk or buttermilk
1tablespoon sunflower oil (optional)

Method
Preheat the oven to 200ºC/400ºF/gas mark 6 and grease a baking tray.
Sieve the plain flour, salt and bread soda into a bowl. Mix in the wholemeal flour and sugar.
Make a well in the centre of the flour and gradually pour in the milk and oil and mix to obtain a dough that is stiff enough to handle (you may not need to use all of the milk).
Turn the dough out onto floured board, knead lightly and flatten out to a thickness of 2 cm/1 in.
Cut into circles using a scone cutter and place on the greased baking tray.
Brush the tops with a little milk and bake in the oven for about 12–15 minutes until golden in colour.

Note: a little topping of grated cheese sprinkled on before baking is a very nice extra on the scones.

Cheese scones

225g/8oz self-raising flour
1 teaspoon baking powder
1 teaspoon mustard powder

50g/2oz grated chedder cheese
125 ml/4 fl oz milk
1 tablespoon sunflower oil

Method
Preheat the oven to 200ºC/400ºF/gas mark 6 and grease a baking tray.
Sieve the flour, mustard and baking powder into a bowl. Add in the cheese
and mix well.
Mix the milk and oil together. Make a well in the centre of the flour and gradually pour in the liquid, mixing from the centre out to make a nice moist dough that is firm enough to handle.
Turn out on a floured board and knead lightly. Roll out to about 2 cm/1 in thick and cut into rounds with a scone cutter.
Brush the tops with milk, place on a hot baking tray and cook in the oven for about 15 minutes until golden.

Note: sprinkle the tops with a little grated cheese for extra flavour before putting in the oven. Heating the baking tray in advance gives a better result.

Index